D0359814

SLANDERING JESUS

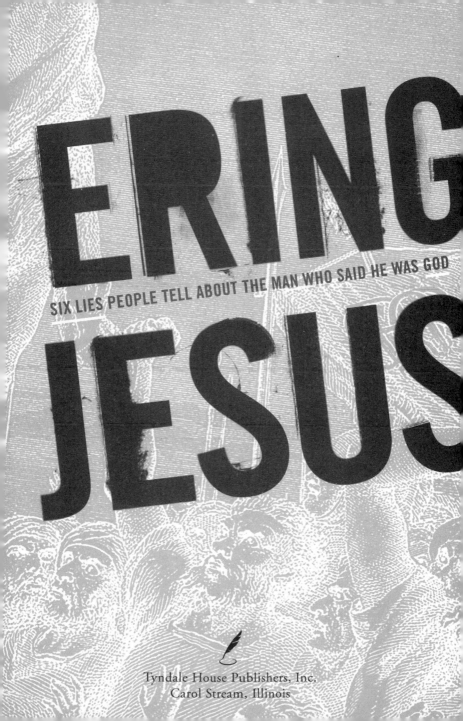

ERING

SIX LIES PEOPLE TELL ABOUT THE MAN WHO SAID HE WAS GOD

JESUS

Tyndale House Publishers, Inc.
Carol Stream, Illinois

Visit Tyndale's exciting Web site at www.tyndale.com

TYNDALE and Tyndale's quill logo are registered trademarks of Tyndale House Publishers, Inc.

Slandering Jesus: Six Lies People Tell about the Man Who Said He Was God

Copyright © 2007 by Erwin W. Lutzer. All rights reserved.

Cover photo copyright © by Brand X/Veer. All rights reserved.

Author photo by Jim Whitmer. All rights reserved.

Designed by Erik Peterson

All scripture quotations, unless otherwise indicated, are taken from the HOLY BIBLE, NEW INTERNATIONAL VERSION®. NIV®. Copyright © 1973, 1978, 1984 by International Bible Society. Used by permission of Zondervan. All rights reserved.

Scripture quotations marked NKJV are taken from the New King James Version®. Copyright © 1982 by Thomas Nelson, Inc. Used by permission. All rights reserved. *NKJV* is a trademark of Thomas Nelson, Inc.

Scripture quotations marked KJV are taken from the *Holy Bible,* King James Version.

Library of Congress Cataloging-in-Publication Data

Lutzer, Erwin W.
  Slandering Jesus : six lies people tell about the man who said he was God / Erwin W. Lutzer.
    p. cm.
  Includes bibliographical references.
  ISBN-13: 978-1-4143-1460-0 (hc)
  ISBN-10: 1-4143-1460-4 (hc)
  1. Jesus Christ—Person and offices. 2. Apologetics. I. Title.
  BT203.L88 2007
  232—dc22   2007020865

Printed in the United States of America

13   12   11   10   09   08   07
 7   6   5   4   3   2   1

Affectionately dedicated to John Ankerberg,
a brilliant defender of The Faith,
a passionate evangelist, and a faithful friend.

"Always be prepared to give an answer
to everyone who asks you to give
the reason for the hope that you have."

CONTENTS

ACKNOWLEDGMENTS

Writing a book is never a solo project, but a collective task with those who help with the research, editing, and eventually the production process. My special thanks goes to Michael Thate, a brilliant young scholar who helped me with the research and writing of chapters 3 and 4. His knowledge of the controversy surrounding the Judas Document and his keen understanding of the Jesus Seminar helped clarify my own thinking so that the issues could be properly addressed.

Dr. Darrell Bock, research professor at Dallas Theological Seminary, supplied valuable information on how Jesus is viewed today. Much of his thinking is reflected in my opening chapter, "Jesus in the Spin Zone." Dr. Bock's new book *Dethroning Jesus* is a scholarly contribution to the debate about how Jesus is interpreted in our culture.

Then there is the great team at Tyndale House Publishers:

Jan Long Harris, you continue to believe in what I do.

Lisa Jackson, thanks for your careful editing.

Erik Peterson, thanks for the creative cover.

Finally, I pay tribute to my lovely wife, Rebecca, who, when I'm writing a book, has to put up with my erratic hours, my constant presence at the computer, and the knowledge that some important matters will have to be postponed for another time.

FROM THE PEN OF AN ATHEIST

Welcome to this discussion about Jesus.

The question of whether or not Jesus was God and thus the only qualified Savior is one that rational people of all stripes cannot ignore. On this, according to Christian belief, hinges not only the truth of the Christian faith but, more ominously, the eternal fate of individuals. Simply put, either historic Christianity is true or it is the most dastardly hoax ever perpetrated.

No one sees this more clearly than Sam Harris, a well-known atheist and author of the book *Letter to a Christian Nation*. In it, Harris acknowledges that there are many points on which he and Christians can agree. For example, that "one of us is right, the other is wrong." He continues:

> Either Jesus offers humanity the one true path to salvation (John 14:6), or he does not. We agree that to be a true Christian is to believe that all other faiths are mistaken, and profoundly so. *If Christianity is correct, and I persist in my unbelief, I should expect to suffer the torments of hell* (emphasis added).[1]

No one can doubt that Harris understands the true nature of the Christian faith. There is no neutrality on these issues, unless, of course, one were to opt for a mere shell of Christianity that has been emptied of its distinctive beliefs and power. Let us agree that Harris is right: If Christianity is correct, he can expect to suffer torments in hell.

Writing to us as Christians, Harris proceeds with equal clarity:

> Either the Bible is just an ordinary book, written by mortals, or it isn't. Either Christ was divine, or he was not. If the Bible is an ordinary book, and Christ an ordinary man, the basic doctrine of Christianity is false. If the Bible is an ordinary book, and Christ an ordinary man, the history of Christian theology is the story of bookish men parsing a collective delusion. If the basic tenets of Christianity are true then there are some very grim surprises in store for nonbelievers like myself. You understand this. At least half the American population understands this. So let us be honest with ourselves: in the fullness of time, one side is really going to win this argument, and the other side is really going to lose.[2]

One side is really going to win this argument, and the other side is really going to lose! Harris understands that everything is at stake in this debate: heaven or hell, paradise or suffering, judgment or oblivion. At death, our faith as Christians will be put to the final test. We will either experience conscious bliss, or, if Harris is right, an eternity of nothingness. And as for Harris, if he is wrong and Christianity is right, horror awaits.

Slandering Jesus is not unbiased in its argument that Jesus is indeed the Son of God and therefore atheists and followers of other religions are "really going to lose." There are compelling reasons to stake our eternal destiny on Jesus, and not, say, on the writings of atheists. Pascal, you will recall, put forth a wager: Believe in Christ, and if He is the Son of God, you have heaven to gain; if He is not, you have nothing to lose. However, contrary to what Pascal says, belief in the Jesus of the New Testament is not a gamble, but a rational decision based on various kinds of evidence.

But who is this Jesus in whom Christians believe? And how is He distinguished from other "Jesuses" in our culture? To my knowledge, we have never had as many religious options as we do today, so many varieties of Jesus from which to choose.

In the pages that follow, we'll examine six views of Jesus. Each holds Him in high regard, but unfortunately, upon careful examination, we find in each case that He is "damned by faint praise." Too often He is well spoken of, but slandered nevertheless.

But before we get into these particular lies about Jesus, we first need to understand the presuppositions that give scholars permission to reinvent Him according to their liking. From there, we can move on to sample various views and show why Jesus does not easily fit into the mainstream of our endlessly tolerant religious culture. He stands above all other religious claims even when He welcomes us to be in fellowship with Him and His Father.

FROM MY HEART TO YOURS

I'm glad that you have an interest in Jesus. Perhaps it is a mere curiosity, or maybe you have a settled opinion of Him as a great teacher, a guru, or a man who elevated the status of women. Or perhaps you have concluded that He is indeed the Son of God, the Savior of the world. No matter what your opinion, we should all be interested in learning more about Him.

This book was not only written for you, but for your friends and your family. I want you as the reader to be able to dialogue about Jesus, regardless of where you are on your spiritual journey. If you are not a believer I pray you shall become one, and if you are already one of Jesus' followers, I hope you will defend His claims with both knowledge and grace. I want to encourage a whole company of Christians to seize the opportunities we have to help our world appreciate the only One who is qualified to save us from our sins.

The purpose of this book is to demonstrate that followers of Jesus—the traditional Jesus—have nothing to fear about the lies that are being told about Him, lies that seek to depose Him and slander His good name. And we shall see that He is just as controversial today as He was when on earth.

> Others said, "He is the Christ." Still others asked, "How can the Christ come from Galilee?" . . . Thus the people were *divided* because of Jesus. Some wanted to seize him, but no one laid a hand on him.
> JOHN 7:41, 43-44 (emphasis added)

Who was this divider of men?

WHO IS THIS DIVIDER OF MEN?

Jesus in the Spin Zone

"I *also* believe in Jesus!"

That's what the woman told me at O'Hare International Airport before I boarded a flight to Cleveland. I struck up a conversation with her because I saw she was reading a religious book, and I wanted to know what she thought about Jesus.

"I'm a Mormon," she said. "We believe in Jesus too . . . and there is only *one* Jesus!"

I kindly reminded her that there are many different Jesuses in our culture, and if she understood her religion better and if she understood Christianity better, she would know that although we are using the same name, our understanding of Jesus is so different that it would be a grave mistake to assume we were talking about the same person!

In the next chapter, we will consider the spectacular claim that the family tomb of Jesus has been found. But in Israel there are dozens of inscriptions on tombs bearing the name *Jesus*. Many men were named Jesus, but they all have to be carefully distinguished from Jesus of Nazareth, a man who made special claims and invites us all to share eternal life with Him.

So the question *Do you believe in Jesus?* in itself is quite meaningless, unless it is quickly followed by another: *In what Jesus do you believe?* The Jesus of Islam is certainly not the Jesus of Christianity; the Jesus of Jehovah's Witnesses is not the Jesus of the Nicene Creed. As early as the first century, the apostle Paul feared that many of his readers might have begun to believe in "another Jesus" (2 Corinthians 11:4, NKJV). If ancient Corinth had a different Jesus—a Jesus without the qualifications to be a Savior—surely that is even more true today.

Living as we do at the beginning of a new century, many new Jesuses are being fabricated year by year; this is the age of designer Jesuses. Often the only similarity is the name; the character traits are entirely different. So your Jesus might not be my Jesus and mine might not be the Jesus of my next-door neighbor.

This book is about a few of the attempts that have been made to remake Jesus of Nazareth into a different kind of Jesus—a Jesus more in tune with the times, or a Jesus who will blend more nicely into the tolerance that our culture prizes so highly. Some of these revisions are touted as being new or previously suppressed when in fact virtually all of these false portraits have been around for centuries.

The Jesus whose biography is found in the New Testament is being treated like putty in the hands of those who wish to refashion Him to fit their particular view of the world. Just take a moment to browse your neighborhood bookstore and you will find dozens of books, with topics ranging from Jesus and women's rights to Jesus and Zen to Jesus and inner healing. Jesus is used—or rather, misused—for every cause imaginable, from gas-saving minivans to religious zealots. I'm reminded of the words of the late Yasser Arafat, who at a press conference at the United Nations in 1983 called Jesus "the first Palestinian fedayeen who carried his sword."[1] Think of it: Jesus was the first freedom fighter for Islam!

"It seems as though everyone wants Jesus in their parade," writes Joseph Stowell. "From gay activists to abortionists to religious leaders to politicians, making Jesus fit their agenda and flying His flag provides a guise of propriety and credibility."[2]

Stowell is right, but we have to ask: How can scholars take the radical, all-demanding Jesus of the Gospels and reinvent Him so that He, like a book on a shelf, is wholly within our power to do with Him as we will? This Jesus allows us to be in charge, never insisting that we come under His authority, never asking us to stake our eternal destiny on His claims.

> The Jesus whose biography is found in the New Testament is being treated like putty in the hands of those who wish to refashion Him to fit their particular view of the world.

No other name has inspired such great devotion and so much controversy; no other person has been tweaked to serve so many agendas. Scholars are writing books not about Christianity, but about "Jesusanity," as my friend Darrell Bock describes it. Learning about these evolving images of Jesus will help us identify the one Jesus who stands above all others and is actually as good as His word.

In fashioning these various false portraits of Jesus, what assumptions are used to undo the shared results of centuries of historical research in favor of a different Jesus? Jesus, I fear, is much talked about but also much misunderstood.

REINVENTING JESUS

Let's take a moment to understand the methodology used to refashion Jesus to accommodate Him to modern times. It requires some ingenuity to take the portrait of Jesus in the New Testament and make it compatible with pluralism, radical feminism, and other religious traditions. It takes some doing to turn Jesus into a harmless man who demands nothing from us and does not require us to believe anything in particular.

Obviously, some assumptions are required to reinvent Jesus. Follow along as we uncover them.

Assumption #1

One way to remake Jesus is to *take a lesser aspect of His teaching and present it as the heart and soul of His ministry*. For example, there are those who teach that Jesus was primarily a compassionate teacher or prophet who helped those who were marginalized, especially women and the poor. Thus He healed the sick, forgave prostitutes, and had particular concern for those who were excluded from the blessings of the Kingdom.

No other name has inspired such great devotion and so much controversy; no other person has been tweaked to serve so many agendas.

That interpretation is quite right as far as it goes, but it misses the heart of Jesus' life and mission. True, He did elevate women; He did model care for the poor and warn the rich of the deception of selfish wealth. Jesus has had an unrivaled social impact, not only in His own time but also today. Think about the profound implications of the Sermon on the Mount and its teachings about forgiveness and fairness in human relationships. And yet if this is all that we say about Jesus—if this were the sole reason He lived and died—we would miss His primary message.

Today, people often interpret Jesus through what Darrell Bock calls the lens of "ideological feminism." The primary contribution of Jesus, it is said, is that He assured women that they are equal partners with men in the Kingdom of God. Jesus is thus presented as the great liberator of women, but no reference is made to His primary self-described mission: to save us from our sins.

> For even the Son of Man did not come to be served, but to serve, and to give his life as a ransom for many.
> MARK 10:45

Let us suppose that someone were to write a biography of Billy Graham and say that the purpose of his crusades was to promote better race relations, supporting this claim by pointing to his refusal to preach to segregated audiences. Of course, it is true that Billy Graham's courageous decision to preach only to integrated audiences *did* give impetus to the civil rights movement. But can anyone honestly say that that was the primary contribution and message of Billy Graham's fifty years of ministry? I think not. A balanced approach to his long ministry would affirm that the heart and soul of his ministry was found in the message that sinners need to be reconciled to God, and that racial equality was an outgrowth of that conviction.

"Isn't the main message of Jesus that God loves everybody?" I once heard a politician say. Well, yes, Jesus did teach that God loves us and we should love one another, but He also described in vivid detail the fires of hell, warned about judgment, and urged His listeners to repent. Yet today a misunderstanding of what God's love entails is used to cancel out everything the Bible says about homosexuality, the value of human life, and the necessity of Christ's sacrifice for our reconciliation to God. Some people scour the Scriptures to find the one phrase or idea they want, and then present it as the primary message of the Bible.

Our generation loves the buffet approach to religion. In a sincere but often misguided quest for meaning, seekers take a sampling of Jesus if it is to their liking, then add insights from other teachers, and compile a spiritual meal that is just right for them. They develop a Jesus who confirms all they want to believe, and because He is tailor-made to their tastes, they tell us they have found the "real Jesus." Whether we are believers or not, we all are in danger of cherry-picking in the Gospels—looking for verses that support an agenda and then discarding, or at least ignoring, the rest.

Oprah Winfrey, whose view of Jesus is the subject of a future chapter, represents our culture all too well. Her view of Jesus might be right for her, but not necessarily for her neighbor who might choose a different path to God. Spirituality is in, and specific doctrines—such as the exclusivity of Jesus—are out. Jesus is talked about, discussed, and often dethroned. He is a tame Jesus who condemns no one, lets us live according to our desires, and is but one more guru who can be sought for advice.

Assumption #2

Another assumption is that *the Jesus of history should be separated from the Christ of faith*. By that I simply mean that some scholars assume that Jesus was a mere man who was declared to be God/Messiah by His misguided but enthusiastic followers. They did this either out of ignorance or because of their desire for religious and political power. So there is a gap between Jesus the man and the dogma that the disciples believed.

Later in this book we will encounter the Jesus Seminar, which is famous for insisting that the grand claims of Jesus were not made by Him but only attributed to Him by His followers. These scholars pay Jesus many compliments, but what they will not say is that He was the Christ, the Son of the living God. Thus the human Jesus—the mere man—stands on one side of the historical divide, and the "fabricated" message about Jesus—His miracles and divine claims—stands on the other.

Today a misunderstanding of what God's love entails is used to cancel out everything the Bible says about homosexuality, the value of human life, and the necessity of Christ's sacrifice for our reconciliation to God. Some people scour the Scriptures to find the one phrase or idea they want, and then present it as the primary message of the Bible.

As Darrell Bock puts it, "What the essence of this scholarship says is: Jesus is a bearer of wisdom, a model, a great teacher

9

and example, but *he stays put as Jesus of Nazareth*. He is not the link between God and man, and even if he is, he certainly is not the only link between God and man. Any other religious leader could serve just as well. At best he points the way, but he is not the way."[3]

As we shall see, this attempt to separate Jesus the man from the Christ of faith is quite arbitrary and contrary to thoughtful historical investigation. On the Day of Pentecost, did Peter—a disciple who was well acquainted with the historical Jesus, suddenly invent a different Jesus (the Christ of faith) to preach to his listeners? I think not. For the disciples there was no difference between the Jesus they knew and the Jesus who was later proclaimed as Lord by the early church.

Separating the Jesus of history from the Christ of faith makes Jesus very believable—so believable that there is nothing significant about Him to believe! Stripped of His miracles, His claims, and His resurrection, He appears as a pitiful figure with nothing to offer us except, perhaps, some pious platitudes we don't have the strength to live up to. In contrast, the Jesus of the New Testament does not let us off the hook; He tells us that we must make up our minds about Him—and that our choice determines our eternal destiny.

Let Him speak for Himself:

I tell you the truth, whoever hears my word and believes him who sent me has eternal life and will not be condemned; he has crossed over from death to life. I tell you the truth, a time is coming and has now come when the dead will hear the voice of the Son of God and those who hear will live.   JOHN 5:24-25

You can separate the Christ of faith and the Jesus of history, but only if you do so arbitrarily, disregarding the continuity of the New Testament accounts.

Assumption #3

We can thank postmodern thought for the assumption that *history is subjective and that one historical viewpoint is really no better than another.* In *The Da Vinci Code*, Dan Brown quotes Napoleon as saying, "What is history but a fable agreed upon?" One of Brown's leading characters says, "History is written by winners." The clear implication is that the New Testament is highly suspect because it was written by the followers of Jesus, who used their story not because it was true, but because it was the pathway to power.

So this assumption claims that history can be fashioned according to one's own liking and viewpoint; it cannot be trusted to be factual and unbiased. Some moderns say we should study history because of its psychological benefit for minorities, but not in order to uncover some "truth."

These notions about the subjectivity of history mean that ancient texts can be reinterpreted according to one's personal fancy (for noble purposes, of course). This has permitted novelists to blur the distinction between fact and fiction. They argue that because everyone views history from the limitations of his or her own narrow perch, it follows that there is no core of agreed-upon facts in history.

11

The popularity of *The Da Vinci Code* is but the tip of an iceberg; similar diverse interpretations of Jesus are being widely discussed and explored in our universities and in pop literature. Alternate theories that challenge the traditional view of Jesus are growing in popularity, and the media makes these ideas part of mainstream culture. Early church history is being rewritten with interpretations that reflect these recent discoveries and trends. History is being turned on its head: Orthodoxy (the historic Christian faith) is now considered heresy, and what was known in the early church as heresy is now considered to be the true Christian faith!

This presupposition that history is subjective has also led to a kind of multiculturalism that insists that all cultures and religions are equally true and we cannot make any value judgments about them. The fact that they contradict one another is accepted because this is the nature of faith—faith is essentially irrational and hence we don't have to be consistent in holding any particular worldview. Therefore, some would say, the quest for truth is wrongheaded. The modern spirit says that we have to be content with the irrationality of religion, trying to find meaning beyond ourselves as best we can.

Let me make one other reference to *The Da Vinci Code*. If you saw the movie, you might remember that near the end, Robert Langdon, played by Tom Hanks, refers to Jesus and says, "Human or divine, divine or human, what difference does it make? Maybe human is divine." So there you have it: Nobody can know who is right and who is wrong about Jesus—and in the end it makes no difference.

It is this perceived inability to make rational historical judgments that has led to an aversion to all historical or religious claims. Mention Islamic terrorists and someone is likely to remark, "Well, they are no different from those Christians who have killed abortionists." Such comparisons, so much a part of our culture, ignore some vital differences. But who cares? In a world where truth does not exist—where there are no shared value judgments and only subjective opinion matters—clear thinking only gets in the way of the spirit of our times.

You realize where all this leads: Given the bias involved in the study of history, nothing really matters; the content of our belief is not important—only the experience of it matters. History is thus reduced to a personal quest designed to help us understand ourselves better. Why not deny that the Holocaust happened as does Mahmoud Ahmadinejad, the current president of Iran?

Admittedly, every historian writes history from a particular viewpoint—yes, even a biased viewpoint—but this does not mean that we cannot agree upon a body of historical facts that inform our understanding of a particular era. In the end, history can be stubborn and immune to the human desire to tweak it according to our preferences. When Paul argued for the historicity of the physical resurrection, he said Jesus appeared to Peter and then the Twelve, and that "after that, he appeared to more than five hundred of the brothers at the same time, most of whom are still living, though some have fallen asleep" (1 Corinthians 15:6).

Paul tells his readers that the Resurrection could be verified by many eyewitnesses who were still living and encourages his readers to go and ask them about it!

We would never adopt a subjective view of history in the practical matters of everyday living. I can't write a check insisting that my "truth" is that I deposited ten thousand dollars if the bank's "truth" is that I didn't! Sober people know that history is not merely subjective opinion.

We must confront the notion that history is too prejudiced for it to yield any solid historical or religious claims. In the epilogue of this book we will expose the book *The Jesus Papers*, which insists that its fiction is actual history. We will show that such philosophies of history are fatally flawed and self-defeating.

Assumption #4

Much of biblical scholarship today assumes *antisupernaturalism*, the notion that *all miracles are to be summarily dismissed as impossible because of the supposed consistency of natural law.* Thus in a world where miracles cannot occur, Jesus is reduced to a mere man—perhaps a remarkable man, but just a man nonetheless. This means that He could not have been virgin born and that we either have to discard the miracles or reinterpret them within a thoroughly naturalistic framework.

> We must confront the notion that history is too prejudiced for it to yield any solid historical or religious claims.

A well-known example of this kind of closed-mindedness will be found in our discussion of the Jesus Seminar, to which I've already referred. To quote the exact words of the introduction of *The Five Gospels*, a book published by the Seminar, "the Christ of creed and dogma who had been firmly in place in the Middle Ages, can no longer command the assent of those who have seen the heavens through Galileo's telescope."[4]

We have seen the heavens through a telescope, the argument goes, and therefore we cannot believe in miracles. Little wonder the Seminar arbitrarily insists that the early church invented the Jesus of the New Testament and that the husks (the miracles) have to be peeled away to uncover the "real" Jesus, Jesus the *mere* man.

In a later chapter of this book we will show that the notion that the apostles fabricated the stories of Jesus' miracles is bogus. The best historical streams of Christianity take us back to the early apostles, who knew Christ personally and received their teachings from Him. Even the Pharisee Nicodemus had to confess, "Rabbi, we know you are a teacher who has come from God. For no one could perform the miraculous signs you are doing if God were not with him" (John 3:2). If God exists, we can believe in His miracles and know that Christ had the credentials to perform them.

Assumption #5

Whatever is new is true appears to be a mantra in today's highly spiritualized cultural atmosphere. Think of the hype that surrounded *National Geographic*'s publication of the Judas Document. Many people assumed that if it was a recent discovery and if it had been "hidden" from the populace, it must contain the *real* story of Jesus and Judas.

The Judas Document has now been replaced by the more recent claims that the family tomb of Jesus has been discovered.

Standing with an ossuary in the background, James Cameron of *Titanic* fame claims that it is not only plausible but "irrefutable" that the bones of Jesus were interred in a similar limestone ossuary. Each year, it seems, we have a new sensational discovery about Jesus that is marketed to millions via the media.

Hype is one thing, sober reflection another. We'll explore the claims about Jesus' family tomb in the next chapter, and we'll find them to be lacking in critical support. And in our chapter on Judas, we will learn that Irenaeus quoted the Judas Document in about AD 180. Although the full text was found more recently, its contents have been known throughout the centuries. What is more, it belongs to a whole family of manuscripts called the Gnostic Gospels that were written long *after* the events of the New Testament had taken place. These writings were produced by enemies of Christianity who tried to combine the sayings of Jesus with Greek philosophy. More on that later.

To a culture with a short attention span, whatever is new and fashionable is assumed to be the long-hidden path to truth, or something akin to it. According to an article published in *Newsweek*, what we have today is "a passion for an immediate, transcendent experience of God. And a uniquely American acceptance of the amazingly diverse paths people have taken to find it."[5] The latest is always deemed to be the most reliable, at least for *today*.

Assumption #6

A prevailing assumption is that *all religions of the world are essentially the same,* so Jesus has to be refashioned to fit into the continuum of religious history. Thus, He is viewed as essentially the same as Buddha or Gandhi or Mithras, even if stubborn facts must be ignored to do so. At all costs the unique claims of Jesus are brushed aside to make Him fit in the pantheon of our culture's many gods.

Consider, for example, the bizarre notion that Jesus paid a visit to India and studied under various masters before He returned to Israel at age thirty. The desire to place Jesus there is so strong that, although faced with contradictory historical evidence, a case is nonetheless made for this "historical" oddity. The question is not "What is the best historical evidence for this view?" Rather, the question becomes "What scenario can we envision that would place Jesus within the grand history of religious tradition, rather than placing Him above all of these traditions?"

I believe it can be shown that all the religions of the world are *not* essentially the same but with superficial differences; rather, the opposite is true: When compared with Christianity, *other religions are superficially the same but with fundamental differences.* That's why it takes so much ingenuity to make Jesus fit within the framework of other religions. The feat can only be accomplished by a radical historical dance in which we close our eyes to important historical data within the context of New Testament events.

Let's survey six views of Jesus to help us better understand how He is regularly slandered through misrepresentations by false religions and popular culture. Then we will be in a better position to see why the New Testament portrait fits both the historical facts and the kind of ministry we might expect from a man who claimed to be the Son of God.

And with that, we begin.

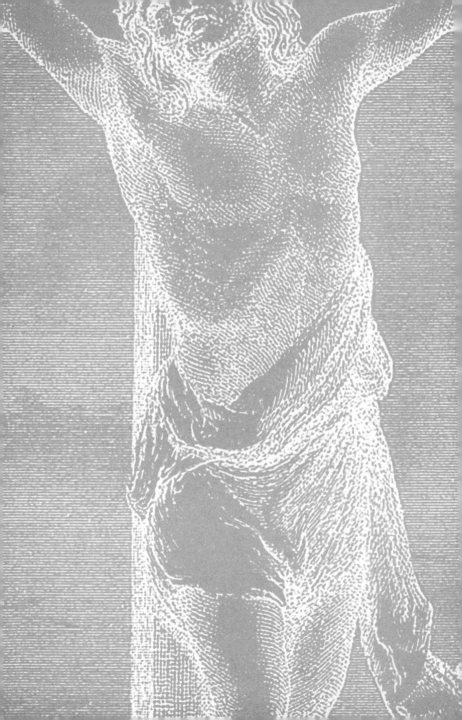

Jesus' Family Tomb Has Been Discovered

". . . the odds [are] 2.5 million to one in favor of the Talpiot tomb being the tomb of Jesus of Nazareth."
—*The Jesus Family Tomb*

The family tomb of Jesus has been discovered!

That's what I was hearing on CNN, Fox News, and MSNBC along with several other news channels. The buzz was that a tomb discovered in the Jerusalem suburb of Talpiot in 1980 has turned out to be the tomb of Jesus and His family. Several ossuaries were found in the large tomb and one of the inscriptions read "Jesus son of Joseph," and four others were purported to have the names of Jesus' other family members.

An ossuary is a bone box. For the well-to-do, the custom was to keep the dead body for a year or so until the flesh rotted; then the bones were placed in a limestone box where they could remain for centuries. So this latest finding suggests that after Jesus died, His disciples laid His body in the tomb of Joseph of Arimathea and then returned to steal His body to keep it somewhere until the flesh decomposed, and that later the bones were reburied in an ossuary in the family tomb.

After hearing the reports, I bought a copy of the book *The Jesus Family Tomb*, by Simcha Jacobovici and Charles Pellegrino. I read it on a flight to Phoenix and then I watched the two-hour Discovery Channel documentary, *The Lost Tomb of Jesus*, that detailed the discovery of the tomb. It was cleverly, and shall I say seductively, presented with the clear agenda of persuading people that the location of the bones of Jesus had been found.

Many people are asking: What are the chances that these authors could be right? And what difference would it make to Christianity if in fact the bodily resurrection did *not* occur?

WHAT WAS DISCOVERED

When this tomb was first discovered in March 1980, it included ten ossuaries and dozens of skeletons, some of them on various shelves along the tomb walls. Because such burial sites are common in Israel, the bones no longer exist today—either having been disposed of or destroyed by vandals. Six of the ten ossuaries in this particular tomb were inscribed, the others were not. Reportedly, the following inscriptions were found:

Yeshua bar Yosef—Jesus, Son of Joseph
Mariamene e Mara—Mariamne, also called Master
Maria—a Latinized version of the Hebrew "Miriam"
Matia—Matthew
Yehuda bar Yeshua—Judah, son of Jesus
Yose (or *Yosa*)—a nickname for Joseph

Let's review these six names to better understand the claims that are being made. The primary ossuary reads "Jesus, Son of Joseph" and would have contained the bones of Jesus; "Mariamene e Mara" is supposedly a reference to Mary Magdalene, the wife of Jesus; "Matia" refers to Matthew, who was a disciple of Jesus but not a relative (no one knows why his ossuary would have been placed in the family tomb of Jesus); "Judah, son of Jesus" is believed to be the son of Jesus and Mary Magdalene; and finally "Joseph" who is listed in the Gospel of Mark as a brother to Jesus (Mark 6:3).

Before I proceed, I should point out that only nine of the ten ossuaries were actually catalogued when the Talpiot Tomb was excavated in 1980. The tenth had no markings and since ossuaries are common in Israel, it was deemed of no special value and left to be discarded or sold.

However, both in their book on *The Jesus Family Tomb* and on the Discovery Channel documentary, the authors argue that the tenth was actually the ossuary of James, the brother of Jesus. If this ossuary, which has been widely publicized, was originally in the tomb, they believe there is even a greater probability that the names are those of the family members of Jesus.

However, we can quickly dispense with the notion that the ossuary of James was originally in this "family tomb." First, it was found in the 1970s—before the discovery of the so-called family tomb of Jesus in 1980. Second, the original archaeologists who found the Talpiot Tomb assure us that the tenth ossuary was simply not catalogued because it had no markings. Third, the dimensions of the James ossuary do not match the recorded dimensions of the tenth ossuary found in the Talpiot Tomb.

Fourth, fourth-century historian Eusebius says that the body of James (the half brother of Jesus) was buried alone near the Temple Mount and that his tomb was visited in the early centuries. And finally, at least part of the inscription on the James ossuary was deemed forged, and Oded Golan, the man who bought it, is currently on trial for fraud.[1]

Facts, however, did not get in the way of the hype that surrounded the revelation that the family tomb of Jesus had been found! The authors requested patina testing to be done on the soot or dust of the James ossuary to see if it matched the materials found in the tomb. To their own delight, they declared, "It is a match!" But the scientist who did the tests backed away from such a conclusion, saying that the test did not *prove* that the James ossuary had been in the Talpiot Tomb but only that it was *possible* it had been there. In other words, the "match" only meant that the James ossuary was consistent with the Talpiot Tomb; presumably it would have been consistent with other tombs as well. The bottom line is that the testing establishes no positive links to the tomb.[2]

Without the James ossuary, we still have five names, all purportedly linked to the family of Jesus. So, we must ask, could this be the place where the bones of Jesus were buried?

Moviemaker James Cameron was involved in the project and wrote the preface to the book on the family tomb. He says that the conclusions of the documentary are virtually irrefutable and stunning in their implications. He writes that the story told about Jesus' family tomb "is pieced together from hard physical evidence, evidence that cannot lie."[3]

So, what shall we believe?

DISPENSING WITH MYTHS

Before we evaluate the evidence, we must dispense with some myths and rather foolish notions that have surrounded this discussion.

The first bit of nonsense says that if the bones of Jesus were discovered, it would *not* affect the Christian faith. Incredibly, I saw self-proclaimed Christians on television saying that if the documentary were true, it wouldn't invalidate Christianity. After all, the argument goes, Jesus arose spiritually not physically. The book *The Jesus Family Tomb* perpetuates the same fantasy by arguing that the discovery of Jesus' bones would not harm Christianity because "the New Testament does not tell us that its chroniclers believe that Jesus, when he ascended, needed to take his entire body with him!"[4] That's like saying that Columbus crossed the ocean spiritually, but not physically. According to these authors, Christianity would not be affected if Jesus did not rise from the dead!

Let us say it boldly: If the bones of Jesus were discovered, our faith would collapse like a house of cards held together by ropes of mist! For one thing, Jesus predicted that He would rise from the dead in His body (Luke 9:22 and John 2:18-22). Furthermore, the whole point of Jesus' death and resurrection is that He redeemed us body, soul, and spirit. Jesus conquered death, and because He lives we shall live also.

Understandably, when Jesus appeared in His resurrected body, the disciples were so astonished that they were tempted to think they were seeing a ghost. So Jesus said to them, "Why are you troubled, and why do doubts rise in your minds? Look at my hands and my feet. It is I myself! Touch me and see; a ghost does not have flesh and bones, as you see I have" (Luke 24:38-39). Then, as further proof, He asked if they had anything to eat and they gave Him a piece of broiled fish, which He ate in their presence (Luke 24:41-43).

Consider the explicit words of Paul:

> And if Christ has not been raised, our preaching is useless and so is your faith. More than that, we are then found to be false witnesses about God, for we have testified about God that he raised Christ from the dead. . . . And if Christ has not been raised, your faith is futile; you are still in your sins.   1 CORINTHIANS 15:14-15, 17

If Christ has not been raised, we are shown to be *false witnesses of God*! Our faith is futile and we are still in our sins.

If the bones of Jesus were discovered, our faith would collapse like a house of cards held together by ropes of mist!

The notion that Jesus rose from the dead with a new body, while His old body lay in the grave, is a modern idea and is contrary to the Jewish understanding of resurrection.

If Jesus' bones rotted in an ossuary, our faith is in vain and we are of all men and women most miserable. We have no hope of heaven, no hope of seeing Jesus—and we have believed a lie. Like the old country preacher Vance Havner used to say, "If the resurrection of Jesus is a myth, then I am *myth*taken, *myth*ified, and *myth*erable!"

There is, of course, a form of Christianity that does not need an empty tomb. But it is a powerless kind of Christianity that is unable to save us from our sins—a Christianity that has no confidence in the final triumph of Jesus over sin and death, and that reduces Christianity to the wishes and ideals of other religions.

But before we assign Christianity to the dustbin of history, we have to ask: How valid is the claim that the family tomb of Jesus has been found? How does the evidence that these are the bones of Jesus compare to two thousand years of historical discussion and research on this topic? More on that in a moment.

We must dispense with a second inconsistent notion—the claims that the Bible should be treated differently than other ancient books. For some reason, when it comes to the Bible, the standard rules of textual analysis do not apply. For example, in his preface to *The Jesus Family Tomb*, James Cameron says of Jesus, ". . . a compelling case has been made that he never existed at all but was a myth created to fulfill a specific need."[5]

He continues, "Until now, there has been zero physical evidence of his existence. No fingerprints, no bones, no portraits done from life, nothing. Not a shred of parchment written from Jesus' own hand."[6] So, Cameron says, this discovery of the tomb of Jesus is doing Christianity a favor because now at least we know He existed! At last Christians can breathe more easily!

The question, of course, is this: What if the same standard of evidence were used for the existence of Plato, Socrates, or Julius Caesar? Do we have fingerprints of these historical individuals? Of course not! Even if we had fingerprints of Jesus, how could we know that they were His? The value of fingerprints applies only when they are compared to existing fingerprints to see if a match can be discovered. Clearly, Cameron's requirement is preposterous.

Do we have the bones of Plato, Socrates, or Julius Caesar? Of course not! Do we have portraits drawn from real life? Of course not! So why don't we conclude that they are but myths created to fill a specific need? *No fingerprints, no bones, no portraits from life. Nothing.*

By insisting on evidence that is demanded of no other historical figure, Cameron has in a single sentence dispensed with both Christian and pagan sources that affirm that Jesus lived and was put to death, and also that He rose from the dead. The shared results of centuries of scholarship are neatly set aside by the demand for a level of evidence that in principle cannot exist.

Given this kind of methodology, we get a hint early on as to how the evidence for Jesus will be treated. From now on, the Bible will be quoted only when it supports a theory, and will be summarily dismissed when it disproves a theory. These researchers are willing to accept a story that describes the burial of Jesus in the tomb of Joseph of Arimathea because it can be pressed into service to support their family-tomb theory, but they are unwilling to accept the next paragraphs in Scripture, which describe the resurrection of Jesus with equal detail. Many such examples exist throughout the book.

Finally, we must dispense with the notion that the Gnostic Gospels present a more reliable historical account than the canonical Scriptures. The Gnostics were teachers who tried to combine Greek philosophy with Christianity. Their so-called Gnostic Gospels were written later than the New Testament Gospels and were known by the early church to be fraudulent. They do not even purport to be historical. Yet in books such as

The Da Vinci Code and *The Jesus Family Tomb*, these later documents are quoted as if they are infallible.

While *The Da Vinci Code* was advertised as fiction (though it purported to be historical fiction), *The Jesus Family Tomb* claims to be sober history. And yet, as we shall see, the authors must turn to a dubious fourth-century text to make a crucial identification of one of the ossuaries in the family tomb.

THE MATTER OF PROBABILITY

So, let's go back to our original question. What is the probability that the Talpiot Tomb is indeed the family tomb of Jesus? In their book, Jacobovici and Pellegrino say that the odds of these names occurring together randomly is one in 2.5 million. The Discovery Channel special modestly suggests that the odds are one in six hundred. Still, these are very great odds that would point to this Talpiot Tomb being the tomb of Jesus and His family.

We must begin with what the authors also acknowledge, namely that the names on the ossuaries were very common in New Testament times. Scholars tell us that there are about eighty tombs and about twenty-six ossuaries with the name Jesus on them. The exact number is disputed because the inscriptions on ossuaries are notoriously difficult to decipher and not all are agreed on. However, to find the name Jesus inscribed on an ossuary is not in itself remarkable, since about one out of every twenty males was named Jesus.

Twenty-five percent of all the women who lived during the time of Jesus were named Mary, which explains why there are six Marys in the New Testament. And among the 233 ossuaries catalogued, the name Joseph appears about 14 percent of the time. So the experts agree that about one out of seven males was named Joseph.[7]

The fact that these names were so common in the first century explains why, when archaeologists discovered this tomb in 1980, no one thought this could be the tomb of Jesus and His family. The ossuaries were carefully catalogued and put into the Israel Antiquities Authority (IAA) warehouse in Israel. Then, more than ten years later, the BBC told the story of the tomb, and Amos Kloner, Israel's most prominent archaeologist, affirmed that these were common names and that it was far-fetched to say that this could be the tomb of Jesus' family.[8] So the report simply disappeared off the news radar, only to be recycled in a sensational book and a Discovery Channel special. The fact that the BBC viewed it as a nonstory should tell us something about its importance.

> The fact that these names were so common in the first century explains why, when archaeologists discovered this tomb in 1980, no one thought this could be the tomb of Jesus and His family.

But the authors of *The Jesus Family Tomb* say that they did take the fact that the names were common into account, and still reached a high degree of probability that this was Jesus' tomb. So we have to analyze their results more carefully. Probabilities are based on assumptions; bad assumptions lead to bad probabilities.

Although the "Jesus, Son of Joseph" ossuary is the most significant, second in importance is the ossuary with the inscription "Mariamene e Mara," which is said to belong to Mary Magdalene, the wife of Jesus. How do the authors conclude that this name refers to Mary Magdalene, since the names are very different?

They argue that some members of the early church called Mary Magdalene *Mariamne*, and the authors appeal to the Aramaic to say that the word *Mara* means "master." They translate the inscription as "Mariamne Master." From this, the fiction is developed that Mary Magdalene was not only the wife of Jesus, but also recognized to be His lead disciple.

But they still have to find a reason to suspect that the name Mariamene is a reference to Mary Magdalene; if this identification cannot be sustained, then the probability that this is the family tomb of Jesus is significantly reduced. To make this identification, the authors turn to a fourth-century Gnostic document, *The Acts of Philip*, in which we are told that Mary Magdalene is referred to as Mariamene. However, when you read the Gnostic document, you find that while there is a reference to a woman who is called Mariamne (though there is a difference in spelling), this woman has no clear connection with Mary Magdalene. The woman in *The Acts of Philip*, is spoken of as the sister of Philip (the Gnostics fraudulently used the names of disciples to gain credibility) and she is preaching in Greek. It is quite a stretch to say that this is a reference to Mary Magdalene.

I can't stress too often that these Gnostic documents are dated later and therefore were not written by eyewitnesses, or by anyone who even knew Jesus and Mary Magdalene. Scholars tell us that the earliest possible date this document originated was the middle of the second century, although the present known copies are from the fourth century. Significantly, none of the eyewitnesses' canonical writings call Mary Magdalene by a different name.

The authors make much of the fact that the DNA in the Mariamene ossuary does not match with the DNA in the Jesus ossuary. This, they say, is further proof that Jesus and Mary Magdalene were married. But the fact that their DNA does not match doesn't prove marriage any more than saying that because your DNA does not match the woman who is sitting behind you in church, you must be married to her. All that the DNA proves is that the two people were not biologically related. No wonder those who were enlisted to do the DNA testing are now backing away from the unwarranted conclusions being drawn from their work.[9]

As I mentioned earlier, deciphering names on ossuaries is a difficult and controversial task. There are archaeologists who believe that the word *Mara* does not mean Master, but rather is a form of the name Martha, another common name in New Testament times. If this is the case, the bones of two different women might have been placed in the ossuary. Also, because the bones of several people were commonly placed in the same ossuary, there is no way of knowing which fragment of bone belonged to whom.

There is more: The inscription "Jesus, Son of Joseph" on the famous ossuary is not undisputed. This is known as the graffiti ossuary because the names are scrawled on the side of the box with sloppy markings. This explains why some archaeologists are not convinced that the name on the tomb is Jesus, but rather a reference to someone entirely different. Furthermore, I can't believe that this is the way the disciples would have treated the bones of someone they regarded as Messiah! Some of the other ossuaries in the tomb had ornamentation—why not this one?[10]

Andrey Feuerverger, the Toronto statistician who did the probability calculations for the tomb, says that his work was based on assumptions he was given. He says, "It's not a secret that the assumptions are contestable. I tried to stay with things that vaguely seemed reasonable to me but I'm not a biblical scholar."[11] Tal Ilan, who compiled the *Lexicon of Jewish Names in Late Antiquity*, vehemently disagrees with the supposition that this could be the tomb of Jesus.[12] Little wonder that Jonathan Reed, who is not a Christian, called the conclusions of the Jesus Tomb "archaeo-porn," the worst sort of misuse of archaeological evidence to support a hypothetical theory.[13] Significantly, no dissenting archaeologists were quoted in *The Jesus Family Tomb* or the Discovery Channel documentary.

LEFT UNEXPLAINED

This novel scenario leaves a number of other matters unexplained. Let us consider each one.

The nature and location of the tomb

The authors admit that this family tomb, if it can be called such, was owned by very wealthy individuals. We have to ask, how would Jesus' family have afforded this burial site? Also, why would the family tomb be in Jerusalem, where His family were only pilgrims? He was, after all, "Jesus of Nazareth." What is more, Jesus was never called "the Son of Joseph" by His follow-ers, but rather "Messiah" or "Son of God."

Why, when these entrepreneurs went into the Talpiot Tomb, did they find a large Greek inscription, but no Christian inscrip-tions, such as a cross or monogram? That tells us that this was not the family tomb of an Aramaic couple whose son was known as the founder of the church. Furthermore, these tombs were kept over a period of decades, so this tomb could contain a conglomerate of people or even adopted family members from subsequent generations.

Who is in and who is out?

If this is the family tomb of Jesus, where is Joseph, the husband of Mary and the supposed father of Jesus? As the patriarch of the family, would he not also be buried here? Even if he had died elsewhere, his bones could have been carried to where the others were interred. And why is Matthew buried here? If this Matthew was indeed the disciple of Jesus, there is no evidence that he was a family member.

Christian beginnings

Even the authors of *The Jesus Family Tomb* agree that the original tomb of Jesus (the one that belonged to Joseph of Arimathea) was empty, but they speculate that the disciples stole the body and later interred the bones in an ossuary. But if this were the case, why then did the disciples proclaim the Resurrection and even die for that belief? Yes, throughout history many have been willing to die for what turned out to be a lie, but there are no obvious examples of those who died for what they *knew* to be a lie.

Think of what this novel theory entails: It insists that in the aftermath of Jesus' death, the family had to steal the body and keep it until the flesh rotted, then they had to buy this very expensive tomb, all the while proclaiming that Jesus rose from the dead.

And what about James, the half brother of Jesus? He surely would have known of the family tomb. How could he have believed and preached the Resurrection when in point of fact he knew that his brother's bones were interred in the tomb?

Also, why didn't the Romans expose these inscriptions to silence the Christians who were proclaiming the Resurrection? Word that Jesus had not been raised would have soon spread, and the claims of resurrection would have proved to be a hoax.

Many witnesses

If Jesus' bones were buried in an ossuary, how can we account for the kind of evidence that Paul presented for those who doubted the Resurrection? In one of the earliest books of the New Testament, written in about AD 52, he writes:

> For what I received I passed on to you as of first importance: that Christ died for our sins according to the Scriptures, that he was buried, that he was raised on the third day according to the Scriptures, and that he appeared to Peter, and then to the Twelve. After that, he appeared to more than five hundred of the brothers at the same time, most of whom are still living, though some have fallen asleep. Then he appeared to

James, then to all the apostles, and last of all he appeared to me also, as to one abnormally born.   1 CORINTHIANS 15:3-8

Paul is saying that Jesus appeared to many people who were still living, so if the people in Corinth had doubts about the Resurrection, they could simply ask those who had seen Him. The Christian doctrine of the Resurrection does not rest with one eyewitness, or for that matter with the disciples—although that certainly would be sufficient for faith. Rather, hundreds saw the risen Christ, and many were still living to testify to it.

Up close and personal

Those who are bent on discrediting the Resurrection accounts like to surmise that the disciples were gullible fishermen prone to hallucinations and superstitions. Thus, they readily believed in the Resurrection based on group hysteria. But history shows that they were actually hardheaded fishermen who were not given to wild speculations or an irrational eagerness to believe in miracles.

"Doubting Thomas," as he is frequently called, reminds us that Jesus is accommodating to skeptics whose hearts are open to embrace the truth but who sincerely believe there is not enough evidence. Sincere doubt is welcomed. It has been said that those who have never doubted have never truly believed. I've also heard doubt referred to as "stumbling over a stone we do not understand," while unbelief is "kicking at a stone we understand all too well."

Thomas had a streak of pessimism, a hunch that in the end nothing would ever come out quite right. When Christ told His disciples that it was time to return to Jerusalem, Thomas said to his friends, "Let us also go, that we may die with him" (John 11:16). He was a loyal pessimist, the kind who would describe a cup as half empty rather than half full.

After the Resurrection, Christ appeared to His disciples in the upper room, but Thomas was absent. Like most melancholics, he likely preferred to suffer alone. As far as he was concerned, it was all over; he had witnessed a tragic end to a beautiful life.

Was Thomas justified in his doubt? The miracles of Jesus should have given him the confidence that not only was the grand miracle of the Resurrection possible, it was also necessary. This was one life that could not end on a cross.

Thomas also should have believed because of the report of the disciples. When they saw Him, they all shouted, "We have seen the Lord!" This would have been a lawyer's dream: ten testimonies, and they all agree! But such evidence was not enough for this pessimist.

Thomas was not the kind of disciple who was so gripped with "messianic fever" that he was seeking reasons to believe in the deity of Jesus. He was only willing to believe if the evidence was beyond reasonable doubt. He famously said, "Unless I see the nail marks in his hands and put my finger where the nails were, and put my hand into his side, I will not believe it" (John 20:25).

A week later, Jesus granted his request. He came through the closed doors and said to Thomas, "Put your finger here; see my hands. Reach out your hand and put it into my side. Stop doubting and believe" (John 20:27). Thomas exclaimed, "My Lord and my God!" (John 20:28). The evidence met his expectations and was convincing.

Is the evidence for Jesus' resurrection just as obvious as $2 + 2 = 4$? No, it cannot be, for mathematics is simply the joining of two concepts in the mind. Nor is it like science, whose experiments can be repeated. The evidence for the Resurrection is rooted in proper historical investigation based on accepted rules of manuscript evidence. The evidence is enough for the honest doubter, but not enough for the dishonest one.

> The evidence for the Resurrection is rooted in proper historical investigation based on accepted rules of manuscript evidence. The evidence is enough for the honest doubter, but not enough for the dishonest one.

Your name just might be in the Bible. When speaking to Thomas, Jesus added, "Because you have seen me, you have believed; blessed are those who have not seen and yet have believed" (John 20:29). We could paraphrase this, "Blessed are you—Tom, Ruth, or Marie—because though you have not seen, you have believed!"

Our faith is open to investigation. We do not give religious truth a privileged position, immune from rational evidence. There are good reasons to believe that God entered our world in Bethlehem, was crucified and buried in Jerusalem, and rose from the dead in a spectacular act of victory and redemption.

From that time on Jesus began to explain to his disciples that he must go to Jerusalem and suffer many things at the hands

of the elders, chief priests and teachers of the law, and that he must be killed *and on the third day be raised to life.*
MATTHEW 16:21 (emphasis added)

To disbelieve this promise is to slander the One who made it.

Jesus Was Not Crucified

"They [the Jews] claim we killed the Messiah Jesus, son of Mary, the apostle of God. But they killed him not, nor did they crucify him."
—The Koran

"No Muslim can pray in the presence of a cross!"

I learned that lesson when I visited Hagia Sophia (The Church of the Holy Wisdom) in Istanbul, the great church that was captured by the Turks when they conquered Constantinople in 1453. This edifice served as a mosque for five hundred years and more recently is regarded as a museum—a monument to the supposed triumph of Islam over Christianity. While we were there, my Muslim guide took me on a detailed tour and pointed out that all crosses that were part of the original structure had been chiseled out. The reason? He explained that *no Muslim can pray in the presence of a cross.*

Jesus enjoys a special status in Islam. He is mentioned in ninety-three verses of the Koran, many of them devoted to His birth. Mohammed himself considered his relationship with Jesus to be unique: "I am nearest of all the people to the son of Mary and all the prophets are paternal brothers, and there has been no prophet between me and him."[1]

Muslims regard Jesus as a great prophet, to be honored but not worshipped. They deny the divinity of Jesus and believe that anyone who believes Jesus is God is to be the object of the greatest curse. But not only do they deny Jesus' divinity, they also deny that He was crucified. *God loved Jesus so much,* they tell us, *that He wouldn't let Him die.*

Jesus enjoys a special status in Islam. He is mentioned in ninety-three verses of the Koran, many of them devoted to His birth. Mohammed himself considered his relationship with Jesus to be unique.

One of the primary portions of the Koran that denies Jesus' crucifixion is found in Sura 4:157-159, where the Jewish claim that Jesus had been nailed to a cross is given an alternate explanation:

> They claim we killed the Messiah Jesus, son of Mary, the apostle of God. But they killed him not, nor did they crucify him. They were under the illusion that they had. Those who differ on this matter are full of doubts. They have no real knowledge but follow only conjecture. Assuredly they did not kill him. On the contrary, God raised him to himself, and God is all powerful, all wise.

So according to the Koran, the Jews did not succeed in killing Jesus, who is called "the apostle of God." Some Muslim interpreters say that the Jews killed someone whom God made to *look like* Jesus. This, however, would make God guilty of deception and illusion. Why would God be party to a deceitful and unjust act by creating someone to look like Jesus and having this innocent person die in the place of Jesus? God would have been guilty of trickery, leading people to believe that it was Jesus who had been crucified, when in fact it was someone else.[2]

Other Muslim scholars say that God raised Jesus up to heaven, and the Jews then substituted someone else and crucified him, in order to avoid a riot among the people. Thus people *thought* Jesus was being crucified, but the Jews themselves knew better. This answer is, of course, false, because the disciples knew Jesus well and would not have been fooled by a substitute.

A highly respected Muslim commentator claims that Judas was crucified in the place of Jesus. According to this scenario, Jesus asked His disciples which of them would like to have His likeness cast upon him in order to be killed and enter paradise. Judas then volunteered and replaced Jesus on the cross.[3]

But none of these scenarios work. Whether God made someone to look like Jesus or whether the Jews knowingly crucified someone as a substitute for Jesus, the end result is the same: The disciples would have detected the ruse and would not have been fooled by a substitute. More on that in a moment.

The bottom line, however, is that in the Muslim view, "the cross did not happen . . . and there is an Islamic consensus to say, 'It need not happen, and moreover, it should not happen. It did not happen historically, it did not happen redemptively and it should not morally happen to Jesus.'"[4] If this view is to be accepted, there should be no cross in Christianity, and the very symbol itself is offensive to devout Muslims.

Where did Mohammed get this notion that Jesus was not crucified? One theory is that he actually got it from some Christian sects, such as some of the Gnostics who speculated that Jesus escaped the Crucifixion. For example, in the Gnostic text *The Apocalypse of Peter*, dated in about the third century, we read, "He whom you saw on the tree, glad and laughing, this is the living Jesus. But the one in whose hands and feet they drive the nails is the fleshly part which is the substitute being put to shame, the one who came into being in his likeness."[5] This laughing Jesus is akin to the laughing Jesus found in the Judas document, where Jesus laughs at His disciples for praying to God the Father.

As we've already seen, these Gnostic texts do not purport to be historical documents but rather the musings of teachers who were influenced by Plato, who taught that matter was evil and that one's goal should be to escape the body. The texts are dated much later than the eyewitness accounts of the New Testament and have fraudulent authorship. No reputable scholar actually believes that Peter the apostle is the author of the Apocalypse that bears his name.

That Mohammed reiterated the common fables of the day explains why he taught that Jesus was born under a palm tree and that Jesus made clay birds come to life. Similar stories from the Old Testament are also fictionalized in the Koran, such as the notion that Abraham and Ishmael built the Kaaba in Mecca, when in fact Mecca did not exist in Abraham's time. Furthermore, a biblical text that is more than a thousand years older does not put Abraham anywhere near where Mecca would later be built. Thus we can safely say that Jewish and Christian history was plundered in order to solidify Mohammed's authority as a legitimate prophet of God who transcends all other religious histories.[6]

42

Although it is likely that Mohammed got the idea that Jesus escaped the Crucifixion from such sources as the Gnostics, we should also remember that the Koran accepts the common Jewish teaching that if Jesus was the Messiah, He could not die. The Messiah was, after all, powerful and victorious. For Him, death would be a huge defeat.

So the argument is this: God is faithful to His messengers; thus God would not let Jesus die. The Koran teaches that God gives victory to those who make His cause victorious and therefore Jesus, as a true prophet, is honored and kept from death. If God had allowed such a great prophet as Jesus to be crucified, His faithfulness and justice would have been compromised. Jesus' message would have been discredited.[7]

However, we should remember that the Koran accuses the Jews of having put to death many prophets before Jesus. So why would God let the Jews kill these prophets, yet allegedly prevent them from subjecting Jesus to the same fate?[8] After all, in Muslim thought, Jesus was only a prophet—albeit a special one, so there would be no reason why He would have enjoyed special protection that other prophets did not have.

There are then two questions before us: First, did Jesus in fact die on the cross, or did He somehow escape the Crucifixion? And second, does Islam honor Jesus more than Christians do by saying that He was so special that God would not let Him die?

WAS JESUS CRUCIFIED?

The Gospels report the death of Jesus with a sense of detail and realism that could only be the result of those who were eyewitnesses to the event. In addition to the Roman soldiers, many people gathered to see what was going on. Two of Jesus' disciples, along with Joseph of Arimathea and Nicodemus, buried Jesus' body, and several women followed these men and saw where Jesus was laid.

The Koran, coming more than five hundred years later, is not an eyewitness account. Furthermore, the Gospels have a number of independent witnesses, whereas Islam has only the word of one man, Mohammed. Nearly half the verses about Jesus in the Koran are about His birth, in contrast to the Gospels, which lay emphasis on His death and resurrection—indeed, Mark and John say nothing about Jesus' birth but describe His death and resurrection in great detail.

> The Gospels report the death of Jesus with a sense of detail and realism that could only be the result of those who were eyewitnesses to the event.

The manuscript evidence for the events in the life of Jesus has been tested by standard criteria for historical investigation and found to be credible. Although this is not the place to detail such evidence, sober historical comparison must give weight to the eyewitness accounts of the New Testament, which have borne the scrutiny of historians, archaeologists, and even skeptics. Muslim claims that the text of the New Testament has been altered are demonstrably false.[9]

Even secular historians verify the death of Jesus. Josephus, writing in the era when Christ was on earth, says that Jesus died on the cross: "Pilate at the suggestion of the principal men among us, had condemned him to the cross."[10] Tacitus (an early second-century Roman historian) describes Christians as those who received their name from "Christ who had been executed by sentence of the procurator Pontius Pilate in the reign of Tiberias."[11]

Additional evidence for the Crucifixion is the way the disciples themselves struggled to accept Jesus' death. They accepted it only when reality forced them to do so, for even they did not think it was possible for their Master to die that way. In his book *The Prophet and the Messiah*, Chawkat Moucarry writes, "If the thesis that Jesus had not been crucified was in the least plausible, his disciples would surely have been the first to support it. But they did not have that option open to them. The evidence was such that they had to accept the reality of Jesus' death. They could not do otherwise."[12] They would not have lied about an event they themselves found offensive, or at least improbable. Peter, as we shall see, especially stumbled over this matter and had a difficult time accepting the fact that his Master would die.

We add to this evidence the compelling testimony of Jesus Himself. Jesus was in distress over His impending death, and it's clear that He shrank back from bearing the sin of the world. The Gospels do not portray Jesus as One who longed to die and hence accepted His demise with emotional tranquility.

See Jesus in the garden of Gethsemane as He struggles with His impending Crucifixion. If He would have been able to escape the Crucifixion, it appears as if He would have taken that option. His apparent weakness was difficult for the disciples to accept, for they did not understand the spiritual anguish He was about to endure. In point of fact, He could have called angels to deliver

Him, but He knew He was on a mission that had to be accomplished (Matthew 26:53-54).

Why would the Gospels have reported an event so terrifying for Jesus and humiliating for His disciples if it had not really taken place?[13] The New Testament allows us to face both the vulnerability of Jesus and also His death, and we must accept both.

Interestingly, even the Koran says that Jesus predicted His death and resurrection. "Peace on me the day I was born, and the day I die, and the day I shall be raised alive" (Surat Maryam 19:33). This prediction is difficult—or rather impossible—to explain if in fact Jesus did not die. All the evidence points to the authenticity of the biblical account.

WHY WAS THE CRUCIFIXION NECESSARY?

The second question begging for an answer is this: Would it have been more honoring for Jesus to have escaped the Crucifixion? Which faith honors Jesus more, Islam or Christianity? How can Christians honor and yes, even worship, a *crucified* Savior? To answer these questions we will investigate the problem Peter had with the ordeal of the Crucifixion and ask, why indeed did Christ *have to* die?

The drama occurs at Caesarea Philippi where Jesus asked His disciples the simple yet profound question "Who do people say the Son of Man is?" (Matthew 16:13). They reply with various answers that they have heard: Elijah, Jeremiah, or one of the prophets. Then Jesus personalizes the question: "Who do you say I am?" Peter replies, "You are the Christ, the Son of the living God" (Matthew 16:15-16). Jesus commends him, "Blessed are you, Simon son of Jonah, for this was not revealed to you by man, but by my Father in heaven" (Matthew 16:17).

Then came the bombshell: "From that time on Jesus began to explain to his disciples that he must go to Jerusalem and suffer many things at the hands of the elders, chief priests and teachers of the law, and that he must be killed and on the third day be raised to life" (Matthew 16:21). Jesus uses the little Greek word *dei*, which is translated "must." He *must* go to Jerusalem and He *must* suffer and be killed and raised again on the third day. This was not the must of logical necessity, nor the must of the inevitability of human weakness, but the *must* of a divine mission. Jesus was on His way to Jerusalem to do the will of the Father.

> The New Testament allows us to face both the vulnerability of Jesus and also His death, and we must accept both.

Jesus wanted to prepare His disciples for the sorrow that lay ahead. The calendar of events was clear, certain, and uncompromising. He wanted them to understand that His death was ordained; it was not a terrible tragedy that had caught the Almighty off guard. Indeed, no matter how excruciating the days ahead, it was all part of the divine purpose.

But Peter found Christ's statement so staggering that he thought he should use his newfound honor to actually rebuke his Master. For all of his spiritual insight, Peter simply could not fathom why Christ, his Messiah, would have to subject Himself to such humiliation. Why would Christ have to die? And even if He had to die, why would it be so shamefully?

So we read, "Peter took him aside and began to rebuke him. 'Never, Lord!' he said. 'This shall never happen to you!'" (Matthew 16:22). He meant well. The idea of a crucified Messiah was a contradiction in terms. He might be able to understand why the prophets of the past had been executed, but Jesus was more than a prophet. He was the long-awaited Messiah, the King of Israel. Kings—at least powerful ones—did not hang on crosses if they had the power to do otherwise! *Peter struggled with the idea that a divine Christ could die.*

Jesus did not take kindly to Peter's good intentions and sharply rebuked him. "Jesus turned and said to Peter, 'Get behind me, Satan! You are a stumbling block to me; you do not have in mind the things of God, but the things of men" (Matthew 16:23). Jesus found Peter's notion a *scandalos*, that is, a stumbling block that would hinder His mission to do the will of the Father.

We stand in awe of this encounter. Peter, the one who loved Jesus and had just pronounced Him to be the Messiah, became the very one who stood in the way of Christ's obedience! Having been a mouthpiece for God, he was now the mouthpiece of Satan.

Peter reasoned that the Crucifixion would count against the honored status of Jesus as Messiah. The idea of a crucified Messiah was unthinkable. But Peter was making assumptions beyond his realm of expertise! How could he be so sure that the Messiah could not die—or, more pointedly, what made him so sure that the Messiah was *not supposed* to die?

Peter's suggestion that the Crucifixion be avoided struck at the heart of God's everlasting covenant. The Cross was the pre-determined hinge on which God's purpose for mankind would turn. Without it there would be no removal of sin, no redemption, no hope of humanity being reconciled to God. This would have suited Satan's purposes all too nicely. Peter's supposed wisdom and the devil's plan coincided. Clearly, *those who insist that Jesus escaped the Crucifixion are mouthing the will and desire of the devil.*

Further proof of this is that the devil himself had already given the same advice to Jesus. There high on a mountain, the tempter said to the Son of God, "All this I will give you, . . . if you will bow down and worship me" (Matthew 4:9). Satan invited Jesus to bow in worship and grasp the kingdoms of the world without dying! Satan's voice of hate and Peter's voice of misguided love were in unison.

For Jesus, however, no other option was under consideration.

> Clearly, those who insist that Jesus escaped the Crucifixion are mouthing the will and desire of the devil.

Despite the horror that awaited Him, the Cross *had* to be. If Jesus had been a false messiah bent on staging a messianic coup, He certainly would not have chosen to go to Jerusalem to get Himself crucified. He would have taken pains to fulfill the popular messianic expectations of the day, namely to stage a revolt against Roman occupation. The fact that He countered public opinion at almost every point confirms His authenticity.

After Christ's Ascension, Peter finally understood the Crucifixion from the perspective of God's eternal purposes. While leading a prayer meeting after being jailed and beaten, he affirmed that various groups had cooperated to crucify Christ: "They did what your power and will had decided beforehand should happen" (Acts 4:28). No guesswork here! The Crucifixion was the plan and purpose of God. It's no wonder Jesus did not call legions of angels to deliver Him; without the Crucifixion, the plan of God would have been aborted.

Jesus Himself spoke of the Crucifixion as the centerpiece of His mission. Hear Him pray to the Father:

> Now my heart is troubled, and what shall I say? "Father, save me from this hour"? No, it was *for this very reason* I came to this hour. Father, glorify your name!
> JOHN 12:27-28 (emphasis added)

We can't say it too clearly: Jesus came to earth to die—the Cross was the reason for it all.

If Jesus had taken Peter's suggestion, Peter's own redemption would have been canceled. Without the Cross, there would be no forgiveness, no reconciliation, and no final triumph over death and hell. The Cross is the hub that holds the spokes of God's eternal purposes.

WHAT THE CRUCIFIXION ACCOMPLISHED

The crucifixion of Jesus was God's finest hour so far as we as sinners are concerned. There the love and justice of God were mutually satisfied, making it possible for us to be reconciled to the Almighty. Love wanted to redeem us, but justice demanded that we pay for our sin, which for sinners is impossible. Thus God chose to take the initiative and satisfy His own demands.

At the Cross, the love of God and the holiness of God came together, each attribute needing to be upheld in its fullest expression. The holiness of God was upheld because Christ's death satisfied God's just demands for sin. John Piper writes, "There is a holy curse hanging over all sin. Not to punish would be unjust. The demeaning of God would be endorsed. . . . Therefore God sends his own Son to absorb his wrath and bear the curse for all who trust him, 'Christ redeemed us from the curse of the law by becoming a curse for us'"(Galatians 3:13).[14] The love of God was upheld because now God was free to extend forgiveness and the gift of His own righteousness.

Follow the reasoning: Since the wages of sin is death, and we are all sinners, either we had to experience an eternal death or someone else had to stand in for us so that we could be exempt from sin's ultimate penalty. Our substitute had to meet all of God's requirements of holiness, obedience, and impeccable purity. As sinners both by nature and by choice, we have no ability to meet God's demands; Only Jesus, who was sinless, has these credentials. To quote Piper again, "If God were not *just*, there would be no *demand* for his Son to suffer and die. And if God were not *loving*, there would be no *willingness* for his Son to suffer and die. But God is both just and loving. Therefore his love is willing to meet the demands of his justice."[15] Jesus' suffering was terrible for the simple reason that our sin is terrible.

Contrast this with Islam. The Koran teaches that people commit sin but they are not sinful. Sin is an act of disobedience to God rather than evidence of a broken relationship with God.[16] In Islam there is no need for God to redeem humanity, because you pay for your own sin personally. Even better, you can make up for your bad deeds by doing good ones. Like a Muslim cab driver in Chicago once told me, "I'm not supposed to drink, but

I do. I'm not supposed to sleep with women, but I do. So I will go to hell, but after I have paid for my sin, I hope eventually I will go to heaven." When Allah does forgive, he lets bygones be bygones because he does not need to have his justice satisfied.

Christianity teaches that sin is so serious and God's holiness so demanding that the Almighty cannot overlook sin. Christianity agrees with Islam that every sin will be paid for; it agrees that the soul who sins must die. But Christianity goes on to say that all would die if God gave us justice alone, for there is none righteous, no not one. The problem is that sinners cannot pay for their sins; only a holy substitute can do that.

So, whereas Islam teaches that we can pay for our own sin and hope that we will eventually be admitted into paradise, Christianity insists that we have an unpayable debt that only God Himself can pay. Phil Donahue, a talk show host of times past, said on one occasion, "If God loves the world, why did He send His son to die and redeem us? Why didn't He come out of heaven and do it Himself?" The answer is that *in Christ, God did just that!*

> Jesus' suffering was terrible for the simple reason that our sin is terrible.

Ergun Mehmet Caner, who grew up Muslim but later became a Christian, says that the concept of shedding blood for atonement is not a new idea to Muslims. He writes that when we explain Jesus shedding blood, a Muslim says, "We *believe* in atonement. We *believe* in blood! The difference is that we believe it is by the shedding of *our own* blood that we purchase our forgiveness. We believe *our* blood purchases our only eternal assurance. This is the concept of jihad—to die as a martyr in a declared fatwa."[17] What Muslims don't understand, Caner says, is that Christ died in our place.

In fact, Muslims object that it would have been immoral for Jesus, who was sinless, to suffer on behalf of others. Perhaps that would be relevant if Jesus had been *forced* to suffer as He did, but He did it voluntarily. It was a decision motivated by love that was clearly in line with God's will.

Far from showing the weakness of Jesus, the Crucifixion and subsequent Resurrection proved Jesus' triumph over sin and death. The Cross is not an addendum to the Christian faith but lies at the heart of it. For there outside the city walls, Christ hung naked as the sin bearer for those who believe. All other attempts to reach God diminish the wonder of that event. Without the Cross, there could be no crown.

In Islam, assurance of salvation is beyond reach, for in the end Allah does with each person as he wills. In the Koran, Mohammed himself said he was unsure of his eternal salvation. Only by dying in a jihad does one guarantee instant entrance into paradise.

In contrast, Christian salvation is a free gift made available through the sacrifice and triumph of Jesus. Thanks to Jesus, assurance of eternal life is guaranteed, for the issue is not the greatness of our sin but the greatness of His sacrifice. When John Ashcroft was the attorney general for the United States he was asked the difference between Islam and Christianity. He replied, "Islam is a religion in which Allah requires [that] you send your son to die for him. Christianity is a faith in which God sent his son to die for you."[18] And that free gift is available to anyone who receives Christ as Savior (John 1:12).

A story is told in Africa that a fire ravaged a hut, burning quickly and intensely, killing an entire family. However, a stranger ran into the burning house and snatched a small boy from the flames, carrying him to safety before disappearing into the darkness. The next day, the tribe met to decide what should be done with the lad. Perhaps somewhat superstitiously, they assumed he must be a special child since he survived the fire. One villager, known for his wisdom, insisted that he adopt the boy; another, known for his wealth, thought he was the best qualified.

As the discussion ensued, a young, unknown man walked into the middle of the circle and insisted that he had prior claim to the child. Then he showed them his hands, freshly burned from the fire of the past night. He was the rescuer and therefore insisted that the child was rightfully his.

The other gods were strong, but thou art weak,

They strode, but thou didst stumble to thy throne

Yet to our wounds, only God's wounds can speak

But not a god has wounds, but thou alone.[19]

WRAPPING UP HISTORY

In Muslim theology, Jesus will return to earth to fight against the Antichrist and He will overcome him. Then He will establish a reign of peace; at that time everyone will convert to Islam, and Islamic law will be implemented in all the nations of the earth. Jews and Christians will believe in Jesus just as Muslims do. Jews will see Him as a prophet and Christians will realize He is not the Son of God. Jesus will destroy all crosses, and this will make Christians realize that Jesus was not crucified. Once His mission is accomplished, He will die a natural death and will be buried in Medina next to Mohammed.[20]

This stands in sharp contrast to the final triumph of Jesus pictured in the New Testament, where we are taught that because of Jesus' humiliation, He has been exalted by the Father:

> And being found in appearance as a man, he humbled himself and became obedient to death—even death on a cross! Therefore God exalted him to the highest place and gave him the name that is above every name, that at the name of Jesus every knee should bow, in heaven and on earth and under the earth, and every tongue confess that Jesus Christ is Lord, to the glory of God the Father.
> PHILIPPIANS 2:8-11

So in the end, Mohammed, along with all other religious leaders, will bow and confess that Jesus Christ is Lord, to the glory of God the Father. Fortunately, Jesus is not only a King but also a Savior who is able to reconcile us to the Father.

Muslims do not honor Jesus more than Christians do; Christians see the Crucifixion as the most breathtaking expression of God's love when He intervened on our behalf, accomplishing what we could not.

> For God so loved the world that he gave his one and only Son, that whoever believes in him shall not perish but have eternal life. JOHN 3:16

Judas Did Jesus a Favor

"You, Judas, will exceed all [the other disciples]. For you will sacrifice the man that clothes me."
—Jesus, as quoted in *The Gospel of Judas*

His name was Judas, the Greek translation of the Hebrew *Judah*, which means "praise." It was a name with grand precedent and charged with prophetic hope (Genesis 49:8-12). His last name was Iscariot, which probably meant that he was a man from Kerioth, a town in southern Judah known for its fruit farms. Whatever Iscariot means, it was meant to distinguish him from the other Judas who also was a disciple of Jesus (Luke 6:16, John 14:22, Acts 1:13).

Let's not forget that the biblical picture presents a Judas who started out life as a baby in his mother's arms, probably inspiring great dreams in her heart. He was also at one time a teenager and probably filled with the idealism, fantasies, hopes, and dreams of youth.

Imagine the joy in that Jewish home when Judas was chosen as a disciple of Jesus Christ, Israel's bright new hope. Judas was now one of the elite, the privileged few (Matthew 10:4, Mark 3:19, Luke 6:16). No one could have predicted on that happy day the despair and gloom that would forever be associated with the name Judas—no one, that is, except the One who chose him (John 13:11).

Judas was with Jesus, up close and personal. He might have been thinking, *Now at last I will be able to realize my hopes and dreams. What an opportunity! What will the kids I played with think now?* His future was glowing and getting brighter day by day. Hope seemed to have no limits.

WHO WAS JUDAS?

But who was this man? The general populace, together with Dante, has long since chained Judas with the devil in the deepest, iciest regions of hell.[1] From Shakespeare's *Love's Labour's Lost* and *Henry VI* to Bob Dylan's "With God on Our Side," Judas's name has long since been synonymous with "traitor." But is it possible that we could have misinterpreted him? What if Judas was not the betrayer of Jesus, but, irony of ironies, really His confidant and covert operative entrusted with a secret mission?

Several books—both in the popular media and in the scholarly press—have sought to loose Judas from Dante's chains. William Klassen wrote a book suggesting that Judas acted neither as devil nor as saint, but rather as a neutral observer.[2] Klassen insists that Judas did not betray Jesus but simply "gave him over" to the appropriate Jewish authorities to evaluate His claims. Judas had difficulty understanding Jesus' course of ministry. Unlike the other disciples, however, Judas thought he would do something about this misunderstanding—he would offer Jesus a helping hand and speed His political reign into motion by handing Him over to the Jewish authorities. After all, pagan overlords could never defeat the Messiah of Israel! Klassen argues that the Greek word *paradidômi*, which is translated in the Gospels as "betray" means simply to hand over—an idea which is quite neutral. Paul used this same term when he said, "For I received from the Lord what I also passed on (*paradidômi*) to you" (1 Corinthians 11:23).

> Judas's name has long since been synonymous with "traitor." But is it possible that we could have misinterpreted him? What if Judas was not the betrayer of Jesus, but, irony of ironies, really His confidant and covert operative entrusted with a secret mission?

But there are problems with this cheerfully neutral understanding of Judas's actions. In the Gospel of Luke, Judas is named last in the list of disciples with this ominous commentary: "Judas Iscariot, who became a traitor" (Luke 6:16). Moreover, the devil is said to have been behind the "handing over" of Jesus (John 13:2). As James M. Robinson, editor of the *Nag Hammadi Library*, has written, "It is very difficult to interpret the canonical Gospels as being on Judas's side."[3] Judas, after all, is called the "son of perdition" (John 17:12, KJV), the same language used in reference to the "man of lawlessness" in 2 Thessalonians 2:3 (cf. Revelation 17:8). Note that Judas and the Antichrist share the same description.

Judas was not simply handing Jesus over in a neutral, disinterested manner so that Jesus could be examined. After the deed was done, Judas went back to the chief priests, filled with remorse, and tried to return the blood money. What he says is instructive: "I have sinned, . . . for I have betrayed innocent blood" (Matthew 27:3-4). If Judas had merely handed Jesus over in a perfunctory move, why would he confess to a sinful act? No, no—Judas betrayed his dear friend, and he knew it.

What, then, are we to make of Judas's motives? At a certain level, the motives behind Judas's betrayal of Jesus perished with Judas. We will never know what he was thinking. What would cause one so close to Jesus to betray Him so deeply? Revenge? Misdirected idealism? Money? To force Jesus to finally act and usher in the Kingdom of God? We don't know for sure.

ENTER *THE GOSPEL OF JUDAS*

The recent discovery of *The Gospel of Judas*, and its popular airing by the National Geographic Society just in time for Easter 2006, has, in the words of *Washington Post* op-ed columnist E. J. Dionne Jr., given "the old, sacred story a dramatic new twist."[4] Some have said it is one of the most important archaeological finds of the twentieth century, rivaling the discovery of the Dead Sea Scrolls and the Gnostic Gospels of Nag Hammadi. Others say it will change Judas's image from villain to hero. And it will also change our view about Jesus—He is not the divine Son of God made flesh (John 1:14), but actually an altogether different being—an *aeon* or emanation that collectively forms the supreme being, sent from the realm above who only *appeared* to be in human flesh in order to teach the secret truths of salvation. He is a laughing Jesus who mocked the Eucharist, and believes in more than one god.

According to *The Gospel of Judas*, Judas turned Jesus over to the authorities because Jesus wanted him to do so, and because Jesus wanted to escape the material world. Jesus wanted to get on with His death, and Judas did Him a favor by speeding up the process.

What are the claims being made in *The Gospel of Judas*? Here are several quotes that will give you a synopsis of its teaching.

"The secret account of the revelation that Jesus spoke in conversation with Judas Iscariot during a week, three days before he celebrated the Passover."[5]

"Jesus spoke to his disciples about mysteries beyond the world and what would take place at the end. Often he did not appear to his disciples as himself, but he was found among them as a child."[6]

"One day he was with his disciples in pious observance. When he approached his disciples gathered together and seated and offering a prayer of thanksgiving over the bread, he laughed. The disciples ask why he is laughing and Jesus replies that he is not laughing at them because they are doing the will of their god. When they became angry, Jesus asked anyone among them to bring out the perfect human to stand before him and only Judas was able to stand before him."[7]

"Jesus says to Judas, 'You will become the thirteenth, and you will be cursed by the other generations—and you will come to rule over them. In the last days they will curse your ascent to the holy generation.'"[8]

61

"Jesus says to Judas, 'Come, that I may teach you about secrets no person has ever seen.'"

"'You will sacrifice the man who clothes me.'"[9]

This last statement gets to the heart of *The Gospel of Judas*. Jesus' body masked His true self, namely His spirit. Consequently, the body needed to be sacrificed in order to liberate the soul. In betraying Jesus to the authorities, Judas helped Jesus get on with the freedom that would come to His spirit after the Crucifixion. Judas did Jesus a favor.

THE TEACHINGS OF THE JUDAS DOCUMENT

The Judas Document is part of the broader collection of Gnostic literature that has received a great deal of attention in the past few years, especially with the success of *The Da Vinci Code*. Gnosticism, from the Greek word *gnosis*, or "knowledge," refers to the teachings of those who believed that they had hidden knowledge. Gnosticism was an attempt to harmonize Greek philosophy with the New Testament. Thus, as a part of this literature, *The Gospel of Judas* teaches the following:

First, there are many different gods. Indeed, Jesus was laughing because the disciples were praying to "their god," but He belonged to a different god altogether. The Gnostics couldn't agree on the number of gods but believed it was somewhere between two and thirty.

Second, in keeping with Greek philosophy, Jesus says at one point, "Your star has led you astray."[10] Again Jesus laughs and explains, "I am not laughing at you but at the error of the stars, because these six stars wander about with these five combatants, and they all will be destroyed along with their creatures."[11] These wandering stars are likely five planets along with the moon. According to ancient astronomical theory, such wandering stars can influence our lives.

Third, this laughing Jesus is not divine, except in the sense that we all are divine. We are trapped divinities, waiting to escape to return to our distant home. Jesus, some Gnostics believed, was an aeon from the realm above—He was not a man of flesh and blood, but only appeared to be human.[12]

Fourth, the Greeks believed that matter was evil and spirit was good, thanks to various forms of Platonic thought. With that in mind, read this next text carefully: Jesus says to Judas, "But you will exceed all of them. For you will sacrifice the man that clothes me."[13] Let me say again that the notion here is that Jesus' physical body clothed the real Jesus, the spirit that longed to return to god (or the gods).

Fifth, there is both an implicit denial of the bodily resurrection and of the church's mission. As already emphasized, the death of Jesus, with the assistance of Judas, is taken to be the liberation of the spiritual person within. The climax of the Judas Document, naturally, is the betrayal and Jesus' impending crucifixion—the great release and escape from this world.

This world, for the Gnostic, is a prison, and why would Jesus want to be raised and returned to prison? And for that matter, why should the church engage in any form of mission? If this world is a cesspool of pain and suffering, our only hope for salvation is simply to forsake it. The vision of Christianity according to

The Gospel of Judas, therefore, is fundamentally at odds with that of biblical Christianity.

The Gnostic teachings have no coherent theology—they contradict one another in ways great and small. In fact, they don't even agree on how many gods there were. They can afford to contradict one another because they are simply human musings for which reason and coherence are not important.

AN EVALUATION OF THE JUDAS DOCUMENT

How, then, should we think of the historical Judas? Should we revise our estimate of who he was in light of recent proposals by *The Gospel of Judas* and such scholars as Klassen? What should we make of the Judas Document? Does it present credible history, or is it just more hype? Should it change our opinion of Judas? No, I don't think so.

> The vision of Christianity according to *The Gospel of Judas* is fundamentally at odds with that of biblical Christianity.

Here we have an example of historical subjectivism pushed to the limit. *The Gospel of Judas* is presented as if it were on a par with the biblical account. But in point of fact, *The Gospel of Judas* was written over a hundred years *after* the historical Jesus and Judas walked the regions of Judea. It is a fictitious account. As Dr. Craig Evans said during the National Geographic Society television special, *The Gospel of Judas* "does not contain any authentic Jesus tradition." During a sermon given on April 13, 2006, Dr. N. T. Wright, Bishop of Durham and an authority in historical Jesus research, said, "This document is worthless historically."[14]

In passing, we should note a common misunderstanding: The media has been cheerfully saying that *The Gospel of Judas* is an authentic document. But by that they mean that it was not forged and probably actually dates back to the late second century. That is what makes it authentic, not that the events recorded in the document are *historically* authentic.

The Gospel of Judas was known to Irenaeus when he wrote *Against Heresies* around AD 180, wherein he said that the document presents Judas as one who "alone, knowing the truth as no others did, accomplished the mystery of the betrayal; by him all things, both earthly and heavenly, were thus thrown into confusion. They produce a fabricated work to this effect, which they entitle *The Gospel of Judas*."[15]

Keep in mind that the Gnostics who wrote this document have no historical or theological connection to either the Old Testament or the books that comprise our New Testament. The Gnostics were at war with the Old Testament God, the Creator. They believed that the God of the Old Testament was not the true God to be worshipped, but rather was an ignorant Creator who created the world from which we must escape. For many Gnostics, their heroes were those who stood against God (Cain, the men of Sodom and Gomorrah), the ones who saw the truth and understood the secret necessary for salvation. The Gnostics vilified the Creator God of the Old Testament, whom they saw as a bloody rebel and a fool. Is it any wonder that they chose Judas to be one of their heroes?

65

Why, then, the hype over this document that even the early church knew to be fraudulent? Dr. James M. Robinson is one of America's leading experts on ancient religious texts. In his book *The Secrets of Judas*, he writes:

> *The Gospel of Judas*, a long-lost second-century fictional account that elevated Judas to hero status in the story, has been rediscovered! But it has been kept under wraps until now, to maximize its financial gain for its Swiss owners. The grand exposé is being performed by the National Geographic Society, timed for the greatest impact, right at Easter. Those on the inside have been bought off (no doubt with considerably more than thirty pieces of silver), and sworn to silence on a stack of Bibles—or on a stack of papyrus leaves.[16]

Dr. Robinson goes on to say, "What has gone on in this money-making venture is not a pleasant story—about how all this has been sprung upon us, the reading and viewing public—and you have a right to know what has gone on."[17]

REVISITING THE NEW TESTAMENT ACCOUNT

The Judas Document does raise a theological issue that we must discuss. Actually, it is a matter that also confronts those of us who believe the New Testament account. In summary, it is this: How could Judas be blamed for betraying Jesus, when Jesus had every intention of going to Jerusalem to die on the cross anyway (Matthew 20:19; 26:2)? In the traditional Gospels Jesus says, "What you are about to do, do quickly" (John 13:27). Doesn't the Judas document answer that question by saying that Jesus *wanted* Judas to turn Him in so that He could get on with His own liberation, His own freedom from the flesh? To ask it differently: How can Judas be culpable for Jesus' death if it was God's plan that Jesus be betrayed to the authorities?

Stay with me as we probe the character of Judas and then answer this dilemma.

Despite all that Judas had going for him, and the grand potential that lay ahead, he had some hidden flaws. These were not obvious to the rest of the disciples, but they were eventually brought to the surface when his true intentions were revealed.

When Jesus washed His disciples' feet, He evidently washed the feet of Judas as well (John 13:5-12). So although his feet were as clean as those of the other disciples, his heart remained calloused and defiled. The feet that Jesus washed had already previously gone to the high priest to find out how much Jesus was worth!

Judas was also covetous. In John 12:1-11 we have the story of Mary, Martha, and Lazarus entertaining Jesus. Mary came with a pint of pure nard, an expensive perfume. She poured it on Jesus' feet, wiping them with her hair, and the fragrance filled the house. Yet Judas was less than pleased with this expression of gratitude. To him it seemed like a waste, so he pragmatically asked, "Why wasn't this perfume sold and the money given to the poor? It was worth a year's wages" (John 12:5).

Don't be misled to think that Judas had a big heart for the needy. We read, "He did not say this because he cared about the poor but because he was a thief" (John 12:6). Judas was a skilled hypocrite. Luke reports that when the disciples gathered together after the Ascension, the apostle Peter commented that Judas had shared in their ministry. Evidently, he had all of the gifts, abilities, and powers granted the other disciples. When they cast out demons, Judas also cast out demons. When they healed the sick, Judas also healed the sick. When they preached a message, Judas also preached a message, and the disciples never suspected that anything was wrong—they even made him treasurer! He must have come off as a trustworthy man. But as treasurer, he pilfered from what was given for the support of Jesus and His disciples. Under the cloak of religion he was displaying some of the basest attitudes and motives. He was living a lie.

Judas apparently was confused and angered by Jesus' lack of political vigor. He lacked the eyes of faith to see the messianic mission of Jesus. He became more and more like a double agent who was consistently a part of all that Jesus was doing. Although the disciples trusted Judas, Jesus did not. He knew the details of Judas's heart.

According to their custom, the group had gathered for the Feast of the Passover. As they reclined around the table, Jesus, troubled in spirit, said to them, "One of you will betray me" (Matthew 26:21). To the everlasting credit of the apostles, they never pointed fingers saying, "I think I know who it is!" No, they did not suspect each other but simply asked, "Lord, is it I?" Matthew reveals that even Judas asked the question along with the rest: "Surely not I, Rabbi?" (Matthew 26:25). He decided to play the game with them; they were genuine, but he was not. He was as smooth as oil.

Trust Peter to have an overwhelming desire to know the identity of the culprit. So he whispered to John, possibly from across the table, "Ask him which one he means" (John 13:24). John did so, and Jesus whispered to John so that apparently no one else heard, "It is the one to whom I will give this piece of bread when I have dipped it in the dish" (John 13:26).

The custom was for the host to dip a bit of mutton within a piece of bread into sauce and give it to the person on his left, the honored guest. At this feast, the honored guest was Judas. So when Jesus dipped the mutton and bread morsel into the sauce and gave it to Judas, who probably was seated to His left, in the place of honor, He was in effect saying, "Judas, do you really want to go through with it? This is your last opportunity to back out of your deal. I am now honoring you and giving you acceptance with the disciples."

> Judas became more and more like a double agent who was consistently a part of all that Jesus was doing. Although the disciples trusted Judas, Jesus did not. He knew the details of Judas's heart.

Judas probably did not even blush. He sat calmly, unperturbed. We read, "As soon as Judas took the bread, Satan entered into him" (John 13:27). Please note in passing that it is possible for Satan to enter a person without a formal invitation. All that you need to do is harden your heart against Jesus and choose to do the devil's work.

Jesus replied, "What you are about to do, do quickly" (John 13:27). Here we have the theological conundrum—is this a command or is it simply permission? This is essentially the same thing Jesus says to Judas later in Gethsemane: "Friend, do what you came for" (Matthew 26:50).

Was Judas simply obeying Jesus, or was he acting of his own accord? And furthermore, why should Judas be faulted when it was Jesus' intention to be betrayed and crucified?

Literally the statement is "What you are doing, do more quickly," or "What you are doing, do faster." What this shows is that Jesus was in control, rather than being the mere victim of events beyond His control.

> I am the good shepherd. The good shepherd lays down his life for the sheep. . . . The Father knows me and I know the Father—and I lay down my life for the sheep. I have other sheep that are not of this sheep pen. I must bring them also. They too will listen to my voice, and there shall be one flock and one shepherd. The reason my Father loves me is that I lay down my life—only to take it up again. No one takes it from me, but I lay it down of my own accord. I have authority to lay it down and authority to take it up again. This command I received from my Father. JOHN 10:11, 15-18

He knew exactly what was to happen and how the events would unfold. The hour of betrayal was not selected by the Sanhedrin or by Judas. And Judas did work faster, probably because he knew he had been discovered, and was likely fearful that the plot would come unraveled if he did not act quickly.

So Jesus only commanded Judas to do what he was already planning to do—to betray the Son of God. Jesus gave him permission to act and to do so faster. Yes, it had been prophesied that Judas would betray Jesus, but in the Bible *God is always presented as both knowing and planning the future actions even of those who are evil.*

For example, what shall we make of those who crucified Jesus? Shall we also exonerate them because they did what was prophesied and thus certain to come to pass? They also contributed to the death of Jesus in a way that was an absolute necessity from God's point of view. Yet in the Scriptures, those who do evil are guilty, even when they fulfill the predetermined will of God.

> This man was handed over to you by God's set purpose
> and foreknowledge; and you, with the help of wicked men,
> put him to death by nailing him to the cross.   ACTS 2:23

Please note: The men who carried out the predetermined will of God are described as wicked! We must candidly admit that we cannot fully understand how God's predetermined plan and human responsibility can coexist in the same act, but they do. The dilemma of Judas, who helped Jesus carry out His plan to die and yet remains guilty, is the same dilemma that is found throughout the Scriptures. No matter how we might try to justify Judas, the Bible consistently finds him guilty and condemned to an eternity of abandonment. *Dante was right.*

Don't misunderstand—we never do God a favor when we do evil, even when God's will is being done. The devil entered Judas to insure that the deed would be accomplished. Then we read, "As soon as Judas had taken the bread, he went out. And it was night" (John 13:30). The darkness of the night matched the darkness of his heart.

The Temple guards appeared, led by Judas. Judas embraced

71

Jesus under the pretense of love—the infamous fateful kiss, an outward sign saying, "I adore You." But by that act he was giving a different message to the Temple guards: He is the man that you have come to arrest. Seize Him! Judas was so smooth that he made great treachery look like loyalty. But in his treachery he showed where his true loyalties lay—with the enemies of God.

Jesus responded with His characteristic gentleness: "Friend, do what you came for" (Matthew 26:50). He did not appear to be angry, and of course, He wasn't surprised. One more domino had fallen into place as Jesus went resolutely to the Cross.

When Judas saw that Jesus had been condemned, remorse filled his heart. In a vain attempt to assuage his searing conscience, he threw the money down in the Temple, into the inner shrine where only the priests could retrieve it. Then he also confessed the truth: "I have betrayed innocent blood" (Matthew 27:4). There was not a single fault in Jesus that Judas

We must candidly admit that we cannot fully understand how God's predetermined plan and human responsibility can coexist in the same act, but they do. The dilemma of Judas, who helped Jesus carry out His plan to die and yet remains guilty, is the same dilemma that is found throughout the Scriptures. No matter how we might try to justify Judas, the Bible consistently finds him guilty and condemned to an eternity of abandonment.

had ever detected; if any man deserved *not* to die it was his Master, and if anyone deserved to live and be worshipped it was his Master.

As Judas watched Jesus being taken away to Pilate, the full enormity of his treachery finally began to dawn on him. He realized that the Jewish leaders did indeed intend to put Jesus to death. He knew that Pilate would most likely grant permission for Jesus to be executed, and now seeing the full result of what he had done, Judas's façade was broken. Judas had enough sensitivity to experience remorse, but not enough to experience true repentance.

Judas "repented," but his repentance was not the kind that would lead to eternal life. It was the repentance of remorse, not the repentance that genuinely sought forgiveness. Knowing that he could never make right what he had done and knowing that Jesus would be condemned to death, he was led to regret and despair.

So as a fulfillment of prophecy, Judas was unwilling to lay hold of Jesus Christ's forgiveness (1 John 1:9), choosing instead to bear his own remorse and guilt. Remorse apart from Jesus leads to utter hopelessness. Judas was so overcome with despair that he did what twenty-five thousand Americans do every year—he committed suicide. Perhaps his perverted mind led him to believe that if he died at his own hand he could somehow atone for his own sin. Some Jews believed that there was an atoning element in the taking of one's own life.

There are two deaths highlighted in Matthew 27: Judas's and Jesus' death. Both died, but only one was guilty. Jesus was deemed innocent even by His betrayer.

In *The Passion Play 2000: Oberammergau*, Judas is depicted as saying:

Remorse apart from Jesus leads to utter hopelessness. Judas was so overcome with despair that he did what twenty-five thousand Americans do every year—he committed suicide.

Where can I go to hide my shame, to cast off the agony? No place is dark enough. No sea is deep enough. Earth open up and devour me! I can be no more. . . . Where is another man on whom such guilt rests? I am a contemptible traitor. How kind he has been toward me! How gently he comforted me when dark dejection oppressed my soul! . . . Not a disciple any longer, hated everywhere—despised everywhere . . . with this blazing fire in my gut!

Everyone curses me. Still, there is one—one whose face I wish I could see again—to whom I could cling.

Woe to me, for I am his murderer. Cursed hour in which my mother gave birth to me! . . . Here I will bring an end to my accursed life. . . . Come you serpent, coil yourself around my throat and strangle the traitor.[18]

Why did Jesus choose Judas? Possibly it's because Judas represents the whole human race. Jesus wanted to tell future generations, "This is the heart of man. This is what man is—he has the ability to appear good on the outside, but inside he is rotten." I've heard it said that Christ took [Judas] among the apostles so that it might not be a surprise and discouragement to His church if, at any time, the vilest scandals should break out in the best societies.

Judas discovered that the gate to hell is right next door to the gate of heaven.

Scattered throughout the Scriptures are many epitaphs. Over Judas's grave we would have to write the words of Jesus: "It would be better for him if he had not been born" (Matthew 26:24). *Judas did not do Jesus a favor.*

So, let us take our cue from the disciples and ask, "Is it *I*?

Jesus Was Only a Man

"What we need is a new fiction . . . we need a new narrative of Jesus, a new gospel,
if you will, that places Jesus differently in the grand scheme, the epic story."
—Robert W. Funk

Whenever I see a picture of Jesus on the cover of *Time* or
Newsweek, I pick up the magazine with misgivings. I know that
Jesus will be dissected, analyzed, and stripped of His deity. The
Man from Nazareth will be putty in the hands of scholars who
are bent on fashioning Him according to their preference and
liking. He will be a no-frills Jesus—a remarkable man to be sure,
but just a man nevertheless. He will be an object of fascina-
tion, not adoration. And in the end, they'll come up with a Jesus
who is not qualified to be our Savior, much less one worthy of
worship.

Thomas Jefferson, the third president of the United States,
was not the first person to attempt to strip Jesus of His credentials, but he is perhaps the best known. Erik Reece, in *Harper's*,
explains what he did.

> Jefferson took a pair of scissors to the King James Bible
> two hundred years ago. Jefferson cut out the virgin birth,
> all the miracles—including the most important one, the

Resurrection—then pasted together what was left and called it *The Philosophy of Jesus of Nazareth* (fifteen years later, in retirement at Monticello, he expanded the text, added French, Latin, and Greek translations, and called it *The Life and Morals of Jesus of Nazareth*). In an 1819 letter to William Short, Jefferson recollected that the cut-and-paste job was the work of two or three nights only, at Washington, after getting through the evening task of reading the letters and papers of the day."[1]

By stripping away Jesus' claims to divinity and the miracles Jesus did to prove them, Jefferson boasted that he had extracted the "diamonds from the dunghill" to reveal the true teaching of Jesus for what it was: "The most sublime and benevolent code of morals which has ever been offered to man."[2] One cannot help but point out that Jefferson's alleged sexual relations with his slave Sally Hemings would not have withstood the scrutiny of this Jesus who gave us "the most sublime and benevolent code of morals."

Be that as it may, Jefferson did in a few hours what is being done more carefully today by New Testament scholars bent on refashioning the New Testament portrait of Jesus. Armed not with scissors and paste but with computers and ancient texts, these twenty-first-century scholars are deconstructing Jesus to create one who is culturally relevant, without the miracles and without the divine claims. Do you find your faith shaken when you read that the very existence of Jesus is questionable? For example, in his book, *The Gospel According to Jesus*, Stephen Mitchell wrote, "We can't be sure of anything Jesus actually said."[3] Indeed, *Time* quotes German scholar Rudolf Bultmann as saying that the Gospel accounts are so unreliable that "we can now know almost nothing concerning the life and personality of Jesus."[4]

Why these conclusions?

WELCOME TO THE JESUS SEMINAR

In this chapter we will examine the claims of the Jesus Seminar, the group of scholars founded by the industrious Robert Funk with the goal of arriving at the authentic teachings and voice of Jesus.

"We are about to embark on a momentous enterprise," said Funk in the Seminar's opening address in 1985. "We are going to inquire simply, rigorously after the voice of Jesus, after what he really said." The plan was simple: Search for the authentic voice of Jesus, examine every source available, lead the historical figure of Jesus on a "dramatic exit from windowless studies" of academic ivory towers, and usher in a "new venture for gospel scholarship" and church.[5]

> Twenty-first-century scholars are deconstructing Jesus to create one who is culturally relevant, without the miracles and without the divine claims.

The Seminar's aim is to rescue Jesus and set Him free "from the scriptural and experimental prisons in which we have incarcerated him." Like a group of rough-and-ready gangbusters, the Seminar is seeking to break into the prison of an abusive warden (the church) who is drunk on his power, and liberate the long-captive Jesus.

The Seminar's method of arriving at the "real Jesus" is rather democratic. Members cull through the Gospels and offer a four-leveled vote as to the authenticity of the sayings of Jesus.

Red: "That's Jesus!"
Pink: "Sure sounds like Jesus."
Gray: "Well, maybe."
Black: "There's been some mistake."

In the canonical Gospels, a mere twenty-one of the sayings credited to Jesus received a red vote.[6] This, of course, is not surprising given the Seminar's beginning assumption that the Gospels are not accurate histories. The process used by these scholars is deeply biased against the authenticity of the Gospels, and it privileges extracanonical sources such as *The Gospel of Thomas* and other Gnostic texts with little substantiation.

These scholars' stated purpose is to change the way people think about Jesus. They have gone public, and national newspapers regularly report their conclusions. They want to "free the Bible from the religious right" and believe that our culture needs a new view of Jesus, a Jesus who speaks to modern concerns such as feminism, multiculturalism, ecology, and political correctness. This is a Jesus shaped according to the spirit of our age.

Obviously, the Jesus they arrive at is a very different Jesus than that of the Gospels. They conclude that Jesus may have only spoken about 18 percent of the words ascribed to Him in the Gospels. To no one's surprise, the group blackballed the resurrection of Christ, along with many of the other miracles. Only politically correct words and deeds survive.

Keep in mind that for centuries, liberal scholars have tried to separate the historical Jesus (Jesus the mere man) from what they call "the Christ of faith"—that is, the Christ of legend and myth. They have tried to peel away all of the miraculous works and claims in the Gospels in order to find Jesus, the man. But many modern scholars admit that this enterprise has been a gigantic failure. They have ended up with as many different "historical Jesuses" as there are scholars. Rather than writing a biography of Christ, each scholar has, in effect, written an autobiography of himself! The life of Christ is a mirror in which each scholar sees his own reflection—his own doubts, aspirations, and agenda.

Those of us who accept the traditional view of Jesus as divine have nothing to fear from these subjective speculations. In fact, properly understood, these scholars actually strengthen our faith rather than undermine it. Indeed, *the Jesus Seminar is just one more reason to believe that Christ is exactly who the New Testament writers claim He is!*

The results of the Seminar are based on several presuppositions that guarantee the outcome of its work. They begin with a rather clear picture of who they think this Jesus is, and then they impose this picture on the texts. In other words, they begin with their conclusions and then find reasons to legitimize them.

Let's consider their presuppositions.

Jesus was nonapocalyptic

First, there is a blatant refusal to accept any notion of an apocalyptic Jesus. Though the term *apocalyptic* is often associated with the end of the world, it also includes the idea that events have theological as well as prophetic significance. Anytime Jesus speaks about matters of judgment or His own mission, He is making apocalyptic statements.

It follows that if you deny the apocalyptic sayings and deeds of Jesus, you strip Him of His right to judge us, and you are then no longer responsible for what you do with His message. In other words, if we cut out those passages that speak of Jesus as Lord, King, and Judge, we reduce Him to the benign man the Seminar wants Him to be.

> Properly understood, these scholars actually strengthen our faith rather than undermine it. Indeed, the Jesus Seminar is just one more reason to believe that Christ is exactly who the New Testament writers claim He is!

Let's take a moment to see how this is applied to a specific text, the parable of the persistent widow (Luke 18:1-8). You might recall that this is the story of a widow who kept coming to a judge seeking justice against her adversary. The judge finally relented and granted her wish just to get her off his hands. This story gets a pink vote from the Seminar: They like the story and think Jesus probably told it. So far, so good. But interestingly, verse 8 receives a black vote. That means that according to these scholars, Jesus probably said verses 2-7 but He definitely did *not* say verse 8.

Why is a black line drawn through verse 8? It reads, "I tell you, he will see that they get justice, and quickly. However, when the

Son of Man comes, will he find faith on the earth?" The scholars blackballed these words with their apocalyptic message because they stubbornly refuse to accept the claim that Jesus, at His return, will vindicate His people and right the evils of this world.

In other words, the Seminar is arbitrarily insisting that Jesus cannot have made any reference to His universal authority, His divinity, or His role as the only mediator between God and man. According to the Seminar, these kinds of statements were supposedly manufactured by the early disciples who chose to deify the man Jesus. The church is to be blamed for making the man Jesus into the unique Son of God.

Do you see how steadfastly they refuse to let Jesus tell His own story? They do not allow Jesus to say anything about His uniqueness; they say such beliefs are the invention of the early church. As you can tell, the rejection of an apocalyptic Jesus is simply the old liberal Jesus rearing its head.[7]

There are no surprises in the Seminar's conclusions. The Seminar knew what they believed or didn't believe about Jesus well in advance of their conclusions. The Jesus they came up with is the Jesus they believed in before they started their studies.

Why do the results of the Seminar have such broad appeal? This largely fictional "real Jesus" of the Seminar "appears to legitimize precisely the sort of religion that a large part of America yearns for: a free-for-all, do-it-yourself spirituality with a strong agenda of social protest against the powers that be and an I'm-OK-you're-OK attitude on all matters religious and ethical. You can have any spirituality you like (Zen, walking labyrinths on church floors, Tai Chi) as long as it isn't orthodox Christianity."[8]

This leads us to a second presupposition of the Seminar.

All supernaturalism must be rejected

Keep in mind that the Seminar's views are based on a radical antisupernaturalism. Every decision is made with an unwavering bias against miracles. To quote the exact words of the introduction to *The Five Gospels*, a book published by the Jesus Seminar, "the Christ of creed and dogma who had been firmly in place in the Middle Ages, can no longer command the assent of those who have seen the heavens through Galileo's telescope."[9] We have seen the heavens, the argument goes, so we can no longer believe in a miraculous Christ. Remember that the much-touted "discoveries" of the Seminar are not based on new historical or archaeological evidence. Yes, the scholars have extensively studied the life and times of Jesus, but only in order to shape Him to fit their view of who Jesus really was: Jesus the *mere* man.

This commitment to naturalism determined the outcome of the Seminar. They found a Jesus who can be treated like a book on a shelf—He can be taken down, examined, and put back without making any demands on anyone. We remain in charge of this Jesus; we choose to let Him speak only when what He says and does accords with our preconceptions of what He *should* say and do. In short, the Seminar found the Jesus they wanted to find. They are simply doing in a more sophisticated way what Jefferson did after hours in the White House.

There is a third presupposition used by these scholars that we can't ignore.

Noncanonical sources are preferred

Without substantiation, the Seminar favors the Gnostic Gospels, despite their late date and their clearly nonhistorical character.

I've already referred to the book titled *The Five Gospels*, which includes *The Gospel of Thomas*, thus giving it the same status as the traditional Gospels of Matthew, Mark, Luke, and John.

Now, I agree that the Gnostic Gospels, such as *The Gospel of Thomas*, are very important sources—not because of what they tell us about the beginnings of Christianity, but "for what they tell us about the interest groups who seek to use them today . . . about the changing directions of contemporary American religion."[10] In other words, the Gnostic Gospels appeal to feminists, liberals, and radical do-it-yourself religionists who want to be Christian without needing to believe in specific doctrines.

Despite all contrary evidence, some argue that the Gnostics were the true early Christians, although they did not believe in the deity of Christ, the Resurrection, and the miracles. Thus some would argue that although the early church regarded the Gnostics as heretics, the reverse is actually true. History is being revised in such a way that orthodoxy turns out to be heresy, and Gnosticism is the true faith!

The scholars have extensively studied the life and times of Jesus, but only in order to shape Him to fit their view of who Jesus really was: Jesus the *mere* man.

And so the Gnostics are viewed with rose-colored spectacles as paradigms of tolerance and skepticism born two thousand years before their time. The reality is much less appealing, since the actual sect was highly elitist and anti-Jewish, and its thought-world was thoroughly degrading to women. As numerous critiques of *The Da Vinci Code* have shown, the Gnostics tried to blend Greek philosophy and Christianity and came up with theological notions that were self-contradictory and wholly without historical merit.

What is the motivation behind these ideas that treat sober historical methods with creative disdain? Harold Bloom, Sterling Professor of the Humanities and English at Yale, says that the Gnostic Bible and specifically *The Gospel of Thomas* "spares us the crucifixion, makes the resurrection unnecessary and does not present us with a God named Jesus. If you turn to *The Gospel of Thomas*, you encounter a Jesus who is unsponsored and free."[11] Tragically, such a Jesus is chosen largely on the basis of personal preference.

> The Gnostic Gospels appeal to feminists, liberals, and radical do-it-yourself religionists who want to be Christian without needing to believe in specific doctrines.

However, if historical research means anything, we must agree with Philip Jenkins: "Despite all the recent discoveries, the traditional model of Christian history has a great deal more to recommend it than the revisionist accounts."[12]

In the same vein, Darrell Bock, professor of history of Christianity at Dallas Theological Seminary, says that we have a rope—not a cord, but a rope—of historical connections with many different strands that take us back to Jesus and the apostles. Thus the traditional understanding of Christianity has much to commend it.[13]

WHERE DOES THIS LEAVE US?

We should not be surprised that the Seminar found the Jesus they wanted to find: a man whose views were compatible with their own, a man who was deified and made into the Christ by zealous followers. Thus the Bible, which is one of the most attested books of ancient origin, has been conveniently dissected by methods that would never be applied to other writings.

Helga Botermann, a classical scholar who teaches at Göttingen University, writes,

> I have been shocked for many years concerning the manner in which New Testament Scholars treat their sources. They have managed to question everything to such a degree that both the historical Jesus and the historical Paul are hardly discernable any longer. If classical scholars were to adopt their methods, they could take their leave immediately. They would not have much to work with. . . . If classical scholars analyzed their sources as critically as most New Testament theologians do, they would have to close their files on Herodotus and Tacitus.[14]

We can say that the search for the historical Jesus is a kind of Rorschach inkblot test. Since the manuscripts of the New Testament are rejected as unreliable, one's own conception of Jesus becomes the only thing that matters. Cut loose from sober historical reflection, many different portraits of Christ emerge: a countercultural hippie, a Jewish reactionary, a charismatic rabbi, or even a homosexual magician.

In the end, we know more about the authors of these biographies than we do about Jesus. Their dizzying contradictions and subjective opinions have led many scholars to throw up their hands in exasperation and admit that the quest for the historical Jesus has ended in failure. Some scholars have had to admit that the portrait of Christ in the New Testament is a whole piece of cloth; they are not able to find the seam in the garment that will separate the historical Jesus from the Christ of faith. No razor blade is sharp enough to carve up the New Testament with any objectivity. Realizing that the search for the historical Jesus is futile, many have concluded that the best course of action is to simply say that we know nothing whatsoever about Him.

Try as they might, they cannot find a purely human Jesus anywhere on the pages of the New Testament. Their subjectivism has left them with random bits and pieces that will not easily fit together. They are faced with a clear choice: *They either have to accept Him as He is portrayed in the New Testament or they have to confess ignorance about Him.* Determined not to accept a miraculous Christ, they have opted for saying that there might not have been a historical Jesus at all.

In my book *Christ Among Other gods*, I tell the story of *Love Among the Ruins*, the celebrated painting by Edward Burne-Jones that was destroyed by an art firm that had been hired to restore it. Though the firm had been warned that it was a watercolor and therefore needed special attention, the cleaners used the wrong liquid and dissolved the paint.

Throughout the ages men have tried to reduce the bright New Testament portrait of Christ to gray tints—to sponge out the miracles, and humanize His claims. So far, however, no one has found the solvent needed to neutralize the original and reduce it to a cold, dull canvas. No matter who has tried to blend its hues with those of ordinary men, the portrait remains stubborn and immune to those who seek to distinguish between the original and a supposed later addition.

Even in Augustine's day, there were already those who would pick and choose the Scriptures that suited them and discount the rest. In response he wrote, "If you believe what you like in the gospels, and reject what you don't like, it's not the gospel you believe, but yourself."

Yes!

As I will show in the final chapter, if we are willing to treat the New Testament with the same respect given to other ancient documents, we discover that it is filled with reliable eyewitness accounts of the life and ministry of Christ. These accounts confront us with a Christ who claimed to be God and had the credentials to prove it.

WHY THIS GREAT DIVIDE?

Why, we might ask, are some scholars able to spend years studying about Jesus and never come to the conclusion that He is the divine Son of God and only Savior? Is it a matter of evidence, or might it be an unwillingness to believe?

In other words, why do people faced with the Jesus of the New Testament not recognize Him to be who He claimed to be? How can scholars study Him and not be impressed with His authority? Why do others not see in the Scriptures what some of us see: Christ as God, King, and Redeemer?

These very same divisions formed when Jesus was on earth. Some who heard His sermons and saw His miracles saw nothing more than "a glutton and a drunkard" (Matthew 11:19). Others saw Him as Beelzebub, the prince of demons (Matthew 10:25), and still others thought of Him as an impostor (Matthew 27:63). In contrast, Peter and the apostles saw Him as the Son of God.

Jesus Himself attributes people's inability to understand Him and His mission to spiritual blindness and an unwillingness to accept the personal implications of believing His claims. To illustrate His point, He healed a man who was physically blind and, in the process, helped us understand the nature of faith versus unbelief, and spiritual light versus darkness.

This story, as told in John 9, is so remarkable that it is best read on your own. But to refresh your memory: Jesus healed a man who was blind from birth. When the man was able to see, his neighbors were incredulous, wondering if indeed this was the same man they had known these many years. The Pharisees, who were no friends of Jesus, were called to verify the healing, and they called the man's parents to see if in fact this was their son who was born blind. The parents affirmed that yes, it was their son, but out of fear they said they did not know who healed him.

What followed was an interchange between the healed man and the Pharisees that is, in my opinion, one of the most humorous passages in the Bible. In a mocking tone, the man criticized the Pharisees for not accepting that he was healed by a man who, of necessity, could only be from God. The drama ended when the Pharisees threw the hapless man out of the synagogue. The healed man then met Jesus and worshipped Him.

Then Jesus said these remarkable words: "For judgment I have come into this world, so that the blind will see and those who see will become blind" (John 9:39). Let's consider the two categories of people Jesus spoke about: In the first instance, the blind are the spiritually needy who are willing to admit their need for sight. Because they see themselves for what they are and therefore depend on Jesus, they are given spiritual sight. Jesus is always attracted to weakness, helplessness, and great need.

Jesus Himself attributes people's inability to understand Him and His mission to spiritual blindness and an unwillingness to accept the personal implications of believing His claims.

But the second category, those who think they see—and therefore reject the light—will "become blind." He is speaking about people like the Pharisees who are so certain that they can see, they find no reason to call upon Jesus to heal their souls. In fact, for now, their blindness is more comfortable than the distressing prospect of exposure to light.

The contrast is between this man, who knew he was blind and was therefore healed physically, and the Pharisees, who were blind spiritually but refused to admit it. Reread this chapter and you will find the Pharisees to be self-assured, puffed up with knowledge, joyless, and content with themselves. So their darkness remains.

The bottom line is this: An acknowledgment of spiritual blindness is indispensable to benefiting from Jesus' healing power. Those who think they do not need a Savior because they are quite fine, thank you, are confirmed in their blindness. They can be exposed to all the evidence available about the authenticity of the New Testament Jesus, yet reject it without a twinge of conscience. Like the Pharisees, they call their sins "failures" and their glaring hypocrisy "imperfections." They congratulate themselves for finding the path on their own.

People like this stand in contrast to those who are only too aware of their glaring need for God's forgiveness and gracious acceptance. These humble, repentant sinners are given eyes to see. The Pharisees understood what Jesus was saying but were not prepared to admit their blindness. With a touch of sarcasm they asked, "What? Are we blind too?" Jesus replied, "If you were blind, you would not be guilty of sin; but now that you claim you can see, your guilt remains" (John 9:40-41).

We could paraphrase His words this way: "If you were blind and cried out for illumination, you would not be guilty of sin (particularly the sin of unbelief). But now that you claim to see, you are still in your sins; your blindness remains." Exposure to Jesus does not guarantee spiritual sight. The brilliance of the true light can make the blind even "more blind," if that were possible. When we are impressed with our own righteousness, we withdraw into our secret deeds, more determined than ever that we will not be exposed as sinners.

"The natural self-centered condition of human hearts cannot believe, because they cannot see spiritual beauty," John Piper writes. ". . . Because they are so self-absorbed, they are unable to see what would condemn their pride and give them joy through admiring another. That is why seeing the glory of God requires a profound spiritual change."[15] To quote the words of Jesus, "Flesh gives birth to flesh, but the Spirit gives birth to spirit. You should not be surprised at my saying, 'You must be born again'" (John 3:6-7). Only those who repent can see the wonder and authority of Jesus.

To quote Jesus again, "This is the verdict: Light has come into the world, but men loved darkness instead of light because their deeds were evil. Everyone who does evil hates the light, and will not come into the light for fear that his deeds will be exposed. But whoever lives by the truth comes into the light, so that it may be seen plainly that what he has done has been done through God" (John 3:19-21).

Not all people are made better when they encounter Jesus. He leaves some people worse than He finds them. The blind are confirmed in their blindness; they now incur the judgment of Jesus. Having rejected the light, they might never be exposed to it again.

Only Jesus can make the blind to see, the deaf to hear, and the crippled to walk. And He does this by showing us our need for repentance and grace. He said to His disciples, "Blessed are your eyes because they see, and your ears because they hear" (Matthew 13:16).

Slandering Jesus comes naturally to the spiritually blind; worshipping Him comes naturally to those to whom He has given sight. As always, Jesus divides men.

Jesus Has a Dark Secret

"Mary was pregnant by a Roman soldier named Panthera and was driven away by her husband as an adulterer."
—Celsus

Come with me to the Parliament of the World's Religions, held in Chicago several years ago, where five thousand delegates from all over the world met to discuss the possibility of uniting all the religions of the world. One morning I decided to walk through the display area to see if I could find a religion that claimed to have a sinless savior, or even a sinless prophet.

I began my search by asking a Hindu swami whether any of their teachers claimed sinlessness. "No," he said, appearing irritated with my question. "If anyone claims he is sinless, he is not a Hindu!"

What about Buddha? No, I was told, he didn't claim sinlessness. Buddha found a group of ascetics and preached sermons to them. He taught that all outward things are only distractions and encouraged a life of discipline and contemplation. He sought enlightenment and urged his followers to do the same. He died seeking enlightenment. No sinlessness here.

What about Baha' Allah? He claimed he had a revelation

95

from God that was more complete, more enlightened than those before him. Though he was convinced of the truth of his teachings, he made few personal claims. He thought his writings were "more perfect" than others, but he never claimed perfection or sinlessness for himself.

When I came to the representatives of the Muslim faith, I already knew that in the Koran the prophet Mohammed admitted his need for forgiveness. They agreed. "There is no God but Allah, and Mohammed is his prophet," is the basic Muslim creed. But Mohammed was an imperfect man. Again, no sinlessness there.

Why was I searching for a sinless savior? Because I don't want to have to trust a savior who is in the same predicament as I am. I can't trust my eternal soul to someone who is still working through his own imperfections. Since I'm a sinner, I need someone who is standing on higher ground.

Understandably, none of the religious leaders I spoke with that day even claimed to have a savior. Their prophets, they said, showed the way but made no pretense regarding their ability to personally forgive sins or transform so much as a single human being. Like a street sign, they gave directions but were not able to take us where we need to go. If we need saving, we will have to do it ourselves. The reason is obvious: No matter how wise, gifted, or influential other prophets, gurus, and teachers might have been, they had the presence of mind to know that they were imperfect just like the rest of us. They never even presumed to be able to reach down into the murky water of human depravity and bring sinners into the presence of God.

How different was Christ: "Can any of you prove me guilty of sin? If I am telling the truth, why don't you believe me?" (John 8:46). He pointed out hypocrisy in the lives of His critics, but none of them returned the compliment.

Judas, an apparent friend turned enemy, said, "I have sinned . . . for I have betrayed innocent blood" (Matthew 27:4).

Pilate, who tried to find fault with Christ, confessed, "I find no basis for a charge against this man" (Luke 23:4).

Peter, who lived with Jesus for three years, said that "he committed no sin, and no deceit was found in his mouth" (1 Peter 2:22).

Paul the apostle said that God the Father "made him who had no sin to be sin for us, so that in him we might become the righteousness of God" (2 Corinthians 5:21).

Either Jesus was sinless or He was the greatest of sinners for deceiving so many people about His sinlessness! As someone has well said, the best reason we have for believing in the sinlessness of Jesus is the fact that He allowed His dearest friends to think that He was.

> I can't trust my eternal soul to someone who is still working through his own imperfections. Since I'm a sinner, I need someone who is standing on higher ground.

Why was Jesus exempt from the sin that is so much a part of our experience? If He had had a human father, the sin nature would have been passed to Him like it is to us, from father to son. If He had been the son of Adam in a natural way, He would have been a sinner. But Mary experienced a miracle that ensured the perfection of her Son. He was like us, but with an important difference.

THE VIRGIN BIRTH UNDER ATTACK

As we might expect, the Virgin Birth has always been under attack from naturalists who refuse to accept the uniqueness of Jesus and who insist that He must be reduced to a mere man. Although these attacks have been adequately answered by sober historical investigation, they continue to recur, usually with a different slant each time.

Most recently, a noted scholar has revived the debate by insisting that Jesus had a human father—not Joseph, but a Roman soldier whose remains lie buried in Germany. More specifically, Jesus' father is named Pantera,* and you can see his ossuary near Munich.

That is one of the major theses of the book *The Jesus Dynasty: The Hidden History of Jesus, His Royal Family, and the Birth of Christianity,* by James D. Tabor. The author has impressive credentials: He is a graduate of the University of Chicago and chairman of religious studies at the University of North Carolina at Charlotte. And as we shall see, he has chosen to revive an ancient tale and give it plausibility.

Of course, a book that denies miracles such as the Virgin Birth makes assumptions. The primary one is clearly stated by the author himself: "The assumption of the historian is that all human beings have both a biological mother and father, and that Jesus is no exception. That leaves two possibilities—either Joseph or some other unnamed man was the father of Jesus."[1] As concerns the Resurrection, Tabor also says, "Dead bodies don't rise—not if one is clinically dead—as Jesus surely was

*Pantera was a Greek name common to the period, especially as a surname for Roman soldiers. The name is also translated as *Panthera* and Pentera, and the different spellings are used interchangeably.

after Roman crucifixion and three days in a tomb."[2] So with that dogged commitment to antisupernaturalism, Tabor has effectively dispensed with the New Testament accounts, neatly setting aside the weight of the historical evidence.

But—and let's not hurry over this quickly—Tabor does make this interesting concession. He writes, "Granted, both Matthew and Luke include dreams and visions of angels but the core story itself—that of a man who discovers that his bride-to-be is pregnant and knows he is not the father—has a realistic and thoroughly human quality to it. The narrative, despite its miraculous elements, *'rings true'*" (emphasis added).[3]

So although he admits that the biblical story "rings true," Tabor goes on to present a different scenario, which I'm sure he hopes will ring true or will even "ring truer." In the process, he reveals the faith he has in an obscure text that has been known for centuries.

Let's follow the evidence and see where it leads.

First, where does the idea of the Virgin Birth come from? Tabor writes that mythologies of humans being fathered by gods were quite common in Greco-Roman culture.[4] So, he goes on to say, followers of Jesus invented these stories to honor Jesus and promote His exalted status.

Then he asks, "What if the virgin birth stories were created, not to present Jesus as a divine Greco-Roman-style hero, but to address a shockingly real situation—Mary's pregnancy before her marriage to Joseph?"[5] After all, even when Jesus was an adult, rumors apparently were still swirling around about the circumstances of His birth. "We were not born of fornication," the Pharisees said, with the clear implication that they thought He had been (John 8:41, NKJV).

Tabor argues that all four women Matthew mentions in his genealogy had intimate relationships out of wedlock, and at least two of them became pregnant. He writes that by naming these particular women, Matthew seems to be implicitly addressing Mary's situation. We should note in passing here that Tabor is grasping at straws, since the genealogy of these women and the story of the Virgin Birth of Jesus are very dissimilar. The inclusion of women in the genealogy makes the point that God makes His choices on the basis of grace and even an immoral woman, or a non-Jewish woman like Ruth (a Moabite) can be an ancestor of Jesus; in contrast, the miracle of the Virgin Birth is described to show that Joseph was only the legal, but not the biological father of Jesus.

Tabor goes on to speculate that Jesus' father might have been the Roman soldier Pantera, based on a story that dates back to AD 178, more than a hundred years after the time of Jesus. A Greek philosopher by the name of Celsus wrote a book against Christianity in which he relates a tale that Mary "was pregnant by a Roman soldier named Panthera."[6] The assumption is that this Greek writer was repeating what he had heard in Jewish circles. So the ancient expression "Jesus, the son of Pentera" is used to support Tabor's alternate theory. Tabor has not discovered new information, as he alleges, but is instead reconsidering a text that has been known and discredited in the past. Donald Carson of Trinity University comments that "although it is presented in the book as this great find that has been suppressed, it's been discussed and carefully weighed by centuries of scholars."[7] Pantera was an incredibly popular Roman name at the time of Christ, and the tale that a Roman soldier was the father of Jesus has already been adequately answered.

So why does Tabor, against all standard historical procedure, prefer a second-century account by an enemy of Christianity to the well-attested New Testament documents? To quote Carson again:

> What Dr. Tabor has done is assume that the whole thing cannot be. . . . Therefore the evidence has to be jiggered, it has to be selectively appealed to in order to take away the evidence of God actually doing something in space, time, history. At that point, no amount of evidence will ever convince him [Dr. Tabor] unless he's open to the possibility that he himself is wrong . . . and that God has disclosed himself in space, time, and history through a man, namely, Jesus of Nazareth.[8]

Once again, Tabor's dogged commitment to a nonmiraculous Jesus precludes the acceptance of the biblical account. In a sense, despite his impeccable educational credentials, Tabor has committed the same fallacy as the Jesus Seminar: He has found the kind of Jesus he was looking for, a no-frills Jesus who is not God's special revelation to man.

So we can see that a second-century account is preferable to a first-century account if one is determined to scrub Jesus clean of His divinity. And an obscure reference is given preference over a clear one in order to make the story of Jesus more palatable to human understanding.

Granted, the Virgin Birth is not easy to believe. But when we consider it within the context of salvation history, it not only makes sense, it also becomes eminently believable. In the words of Tabor himself, the biblical account "rings true."

REASONS FOR THE VIRGIN BIRTH

Let's review this bit of theology: When Adam sinned, the whole human race was involved. Just like the mighty oak tree is in the acorn, so all of us were in Adam and we inherited his sinfulness. Paul made it clear that not only did we all sin in Adam, but through him we are also all sinners by nature. Because of the Virgin Birth, however, Jesus was not fully descended from Adam, and this break in the line of descent was the means God chose to preserve His sinlessness.

Granted, the Virgin Birth is not easy to believe. But when we consider it within the context of salvation history, it not only makes sense, it also becomes eminently believable.

No detail is overlooked in making us understand that Christ was virgin born. In Matthew's genealogy he writes, "Jacob the father of Joseph, the husband of Mary, *of whom* was born Jesus, who is called Christ" (Matthew 1:16, emphasis added). In English, the pronoun *whom* can refer to either a man or a woman, but the Greek language specifies the gender. Although in Jewish tradition the genealogy is always passed through the father and not the mother, the phrase *of whom* used here is feminine. Matthew wants to be clear that Christ did not have a human father.

Then the account continues: "This is how the birth of Jesus Christ came about: His mother Mary was pledged to be married to Joseph, but before they came together, she was found to be with child through the Holy Spirit" (Matthew 1:18; see also Matthew 1:25).

Luke records Mary's response: "'How will this be,' Mary asked the angel, 'since I am a virgin?' The angel answered, 'The Holy Spirit will come upon you, and the power of the Most High will overshadow you. So the holy one to be born will be called the Son of God'" (Luke 1:34-35). Please notice how Luke makes a direct connection between the Virgin Birth and the sinlessness of Jesus. The unborn child was already holy!

But might not Jesus have been born as an ordinary child, and then at a later time (perhaps at His baptism) become infused with the divine nature? That's been suggested, but this theory poses another question: "What would have happened to the sins He had committed prior to this transformation?" No, Christ did not progress from sinner to sainthood in His spiritual journey. He was the same person He always was: the sinless Son of God.

Others have argued that if Christ had had a human father, God still could have done a miracle and made Him sinless. Since God is capable of all kinds of miracles, that is possible. But some scholars have pointed out, quite rightly, that a sinless man in the moral realm would be a greater miracle than the Virgin Birth in the biological realm.

> Luke makes a direct connection between the Virgin Birth and the sinlessness of Jesus. The unborn child was already holy!

God, I'm sure, could have preserved Christ's sinlessness in different ways, but He chose to accomplish this through a virgin conception. The fetus is described as a "holy child," words that cannot apply to any one of us. Like us, Jesus was conceived in a woman—but without sin. The Incarnation took place in the womb of Mary.

Needless to say, Tabor is not the first scholar to deny the Virgin Birth. Many have tried to strip Christ of His credentials to be a Savior; they insist that He was only a man—capable of pointing us toward ethical ideals—but no more qualified than we are to lift us out of our own sinfulness.

Maybe you have struggled with your belief in the Virgin Birth. You may have heard that it is based on ancient mythologies found in other religions and diverse pagan legends. Let's survey some of the objections and see whether they make sense.

ANSWERING OBJECTIONS

Since the attack against the Virgin Birth has had a long history, we need to consider the objections in more detail. Opposition to this doctrine began early in the history of the church and continues today. We'll take a look at several of these arguments.

The accounts were borrowed from mythology

Like Tabor, other scholars have also suggested that the New Testament writers borrowed from the pagan mythologies of their day. They argue that great people always had a supernatural birth attributed to them. For example, it was said that Zeus was father of the gods and men, and he is represented as begetting children with human mothers. Diana was beloved of Zeus and conceived a child by a shower of gold, which descended upon her in seclusion; as a result, Perseus was born. Hercules was also the child of Zeus, who impregnated a mortal woman. Rumor even had it that the god Apollo fathered Plato.

There is a myth that Alexander the Great also had an unusual birth. When his mother's marriage was consummated, a thunderbolt struck her womb, the story goes. Her husband, Philip, was required to seal up her womb but she conceived and bore Alexander.

Could pagan mythology have inspired Matthew and Luke to tell a tale about the miraculous conception of Jesus? Did these authors have a reason to attribute such stories to Christ? Don't answer until you think it through.

It's worth noting that the pagan rumors about the gods impregnating women arose after individuals became famous. There are no documents that purport to have claimed such miracles at the time of the birth itself. In contrast, Christ's virgin conception was *predicted*.

These pagan legends grew out of polytheism, the belief that there are many gods—powerful beings with human lusts, jealousies, and hatreds; the context was always sexuality and fertility. In mythology, the gods enjoyed human sexual pleasures; in fact when the orgies were finished, the women could no longer be classified as virgins.

Is it feasible that the church would have borrowed ideas from pagan mythology at its most degrading point? Would the writers have incorporated the polytheistic notions of pagans whom they perceived as enemies of the Jewish/Christian teachings?

Matthew and Luke would never have written their narratives to show that Christ was just like other pagan heroes!

The thought that God found Mary sexually desirable is reprehensible and contrary to the whole spirit of the Gospel writers. These narratives are, to quote the words of Robert Gromacki, "bathed in holiness." There is a moral and ethical gulf that separates the New Testament accounts from pagan mythology.

In contrast to pagan legends, the New Testament writers were sober and restrained, and they clearly intended that they be taken literally. The birth narratives are understated and have dignity, plausibility, and a high moral character.

The early Christians had a passion to spread the Christian faith. They certainly would not have encumbered the narratives about Christ with a shoddy story that no one would believe. They believed in the Virgin Birth, and others did too, because it had the earmarks of authenticity. It's not the similarities with mythology that impress us, it is the dissimilarities.

Let's take a closer look at a contemporary version of the theory that the Virgin Birth was made up by the Gospel writers.

The accounts have a hidden meaning

John Shelby Spong is the retired bishop of the Episcopal Diocese of Newark, New Jersey. His book *Born of a Woman: A Bishop Rethinks the Virgin Birth and the Treatment of Women by a Male-Dominated Church*, is another attempt to, in his words, "rescue the Bible from fundamentalists." He argues that 1) the birth narratives in the New Testament are fanciful stories not to be taken literally; 2) Mary was quite likely the victim of rape; 3) the Virgin Birth has contributed immeasurably to an artificial and destructive view of women, because it has been used to force women to fit into the stereotyped role of motherhood; and 4) Jesus was quite probably married, most likely to Mary Magdalene.[9]

Spong grew up as a biblical fundamentalist, loving the Bible with his very being. When he abandoned fundamentalism, he did not stop loving the Bible, he says, but he simply ceased interpreting it literally. To hear him tell it, this nonliteral method has given him a new appreciation for the Bible's deeper meaning!

So, we must ask, did the authors of the Gospel accounts simply intend to "probe, tease, and dissect the sacred story looking for hidden meanings, filling in blanks, and seeking clues to yet-to-be-revealed truth," as Spong says?[10] He argues that the original readers of the Gospels would have understood that these were fanciful stories, but that a generation hundreds of years later—separated from Jewish religious roots and with a Western mind-set—thinks that the accounts either have to be taken literally or must be considered overt lies.

"There was nothing objective about the Gospel tradition. These were not biographies. They were books to inspire faith," Spong writes.[11] Matthew and Luke weren't lying, because they knew (or at least thought) that nobody would interpret their words as fact.

Spong is wrong, very wrong, about his assumptions. He says that the New Testament writers were actually writing comments about the Scriptures, loose observations they knew to be legends. But any impartial student of the New Testament would agree that the authors intended to write a straightforward account of what happened, not a fanciful story to evoke awe and wonder.

They were not commenting on Scripture, they were writing it (see Luke 1:1-4).

Spong does what many liberal theologians do—namely, he rewrites history in order to make it come out according to his liking. This kind of revisionism is not merely done by those who are interested in advancing a given political theory (Marxism, for example), but also by those who promote a certain religious bent. To revise history if new historical facts have come to light is one thing; to do it because of certain personal presuppositions is quite another.

Any impartial student of the New Testament would agree that the authors intended to write a straightforward account of what happened, not a fanciful story to evoke awe and wonder. They were not commenting on Scripture, they were writing it.

Here we have the same dilemma liberals have always had to confront: After stripping Christ of His credentials as a Savior, they are left with nothing worth believing. Spong began by saying that the Virgin Birth was never intended to be taken literally, but was meant only to inspire faith. But faith in what?

He says the account was written to "inspire and create awe and wonder," but as for me, the awe and wonder evaporate very quickly if the accounts are not true. We are left with a Christ whose father was a rapist, a Christ who was probably married, and a Christ who is a sinner just like the rest of us. We certainly don't have a Savior.

This is not scholarship, this is unbelief. Spong is absolutely insistent that the Jesus of the Gospels be reduced to a mere man. He has chosen to deny the Virgin Birth (and other miracles) simply to make the accounts conform to his own beliefs. He denies the Virgin Birth because he denies the Incarnation, or at least he reinterprets it in order to empty it of its significance. His conclusions are based on what he believes God did not do.

Belief in the Virgin Birth is not a matter of interpretation. The Bible is not a book that can be interpreted in any way one chooses. Certainly there is honest disagreement over some texts and even issues of doctrine. But the Virgin Birth and Christ's miracles are clear and unambiguous. The question is this: Are we willing to believe them? Unbelief, not an evenhanded attempt at interpretation, is what has driven Spong to his conclusions.

Spong's agenda comes through clearly on every page of his writings. His book tells me nothing worthy of Christ, but much about himself. For example, I know that he is in favor of gay rights, because in a previous book, *Rescuing the Bible from Fundamentalism*, he argues for more tolerance toward the gay community and suggests that the apostle Paul was a homosexual.[12] I also know that he is a feminist, because he says the Virgin Birth is partly to blame for the suppression of women (presumably because it gives the impression that child rearing is a high calling). I also know how much he dislikes fundamentalists, and how much he likes giving everything a sexual twist. I also know how much (or how little) he believes.

Spong has taken the Jesus of the New Testament and made Him fit into his own personal notion of what Jesus should be. In his book, I meet Spong, but I do not meet Christ. Unwittingly, the bishop has simply written his own biography!

In discussing his views, Spong writes, "The day has passed for me when, in the name of tolerance to the religious insecurities, I will allow *my* Christ to be defined inside a killing literalism" (emphasis mine).[13] He says he will not subject his Christ to literal interpretations. But who is this Christ? How do we know that his Christ is the right one? Obviously he has created his own private Jesus who is not accessible to everyone. Spong should have entitled his book, *My Very Own Jesus—The Private Beliefs of a Bishop Now Made Public.*

In a perceptive critique, N. T. Wright has shown that Spong has cut himself off from all serious historical study in order to open himself up to "a world where the modern exegete can construct a fantasy-history in the interests of a current ideology, in Spong's case a resolute insistence of bringing issues of sexuality into everything."[14] At last he has come full circle: Having assumed that Matthew and Luke invented stories to reflect their own ideologies, Spong now invents stories to promote his own ideologies.

If Spong thinks that his books will "rescue Jesus from the fundamentalists" (that's probably us, friends), he should know that these tired objections to a miraculous Christ have been answered many times by capable scholars. To think that his book will extinguish the faith of true believers is to believe that one can put out a fire with straw!

JESUS REVISITED

We find it hard to believe that the mother of Alexander the Great became pregnant when she was struck by a thunderbolt, not only because the story has the ring of legend, but also because there is nothing else in the life of Alexander to suggest that he was anything more than a man. No historian attributes to him the ability to forgive sins or raise the dead.

But when we think of Christ's death and resurrection, our closed view of the universe breaks open. Unbelief is squeezed from our hearts and we are brought to the realization that this miracle is consistent with the rest of Christ's career. The more we know of Christ, the more reasonable the virgin conception becomes.

The Virgin Birth and Christ's mission as a Savior are linked in the angel's message to Joseph. Mary would conceive a son by the Holy Spirit and "give him the name Jesus, because he will save his people from their sins" (Matthew 1:21). His name was Jesus, which means "Jehovah is salvation." And His credentials enabled Him to live up to His name.

I'm told that in a particular cemetery there is a tombstone that reads: "Sacred to the memory of Methuselah Koking, died at 6 months." With a name like that we would have expected a long life, but among mortals, even the best of names does not guarantee the best of lives. Christ was given a name that conveyed awesome credentials, and He does not disappoint us.

Scan the religious horizons. Go to the library and read all about the great religious teachers of history. Read not simply what they taught but also what they had to say about themselves. Look not for a prophet, for their names are legion, but find a Savior—a qualified sinless Savior. You will discover that Christ has no competitors. If there were another who claimed sinlessness, we would be glad to check out his credentials to see how they compare with Christ's. Mention the requirement of sinlessness and the religious field clears, and only one Man is left standing. Christ lives up to His name!

"Such a high priest meets our need—one who is holy, blameless, pure, set apart from sinners, exalted above the heavens. Unlike the other high priests, he does not need to offer sacrifices day after day, first for his own sins, and then for the sins of the people. He sacrificed for their sins once for all when he offered himself" (Hebrews 7:26-27).

> Mention the requirement of sinlessness and the religious field clears, and only one Man is left standing. Christ lives up to His name!

What is the result of this perfect sacrifice? "Therefore he is able to save completely those who come to God through him, because he always lives to intercede for them" (Hebrews 7:25). Christ is not only able to save great sinners but to save them completely, or eternally. And who benefits from His salvation? Given what we know about Him, it makes sense that it is limited to those who "come to God through Him."

Now we understand why Christ is the only way; no one else qualifies. We also understand why other religions can have prophets, but they cannot have a Savior. The various other religious leaders of the world are drowning men who are shouting swimming instructions to other weak and drowning men.

Napoleon may not have understood the full implication of his words, but he is quoted as saying that there is an eternity of difference between Christ and other men. And that difference, I might add, is that Christ has the credentials of "Saviorhood."

What a tragedy to know Shakespeare as a person, but not as a man of literature; to know Newton, but not as a scientist. But an even greater, eternal tragedy it would be to know Christ as a friend, a prophet, and a miracle worker, but not as a Savior.

Spong's Christ stands in need of the very grace He claims to have brought to us. A sinful Savior is an oxymoron.

But the Christ of the New Testament does not simply throw us a life vest; He personally lifts us from the morally polluted waters found within our hearts and environment.

To love Him is not enough. To admire Him is not enough. We must trust Him with our souls—with our eternal souls.

Many prophets, but only one Savior.[15]

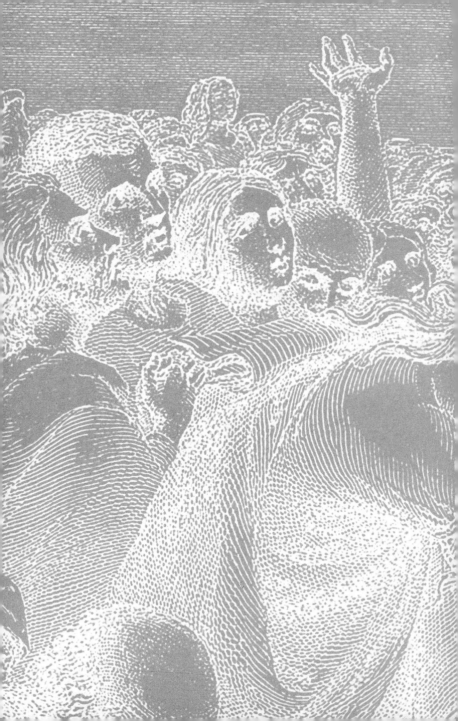

Jesus Is One Way among Many

"One of the biggest mistakes we make is to believe that there is only one way to live. There are many ways, many paths to what you call God."
—Oprah Winfrey

"There are many diverse paths leading to God."

I've heard it many times, and so have you. You're having a discussion with a friend about religion, talking about the necessity of Jesus, and without taking a second breath, the words flow so easily from his or her mouth. "That's fine for you, but there are many ways to the divine!" But saying it does not make it true. In fact, you can be quite sure that those who repeat this politically correct mantra do not understand the gospel. This chapter will help us understand why the only way to God is through Jesus and why there *cannot* be other ways. Stay with me on this one.

Since Oprah Winfrey is one of the most popular proponents of the "Jesus is one way among many" philosophy, let's take a moment to analyze her spiritual teachings so we better understand what she believes about Jesus. After all, she is considered by millions as one of America's most respected and admired spiritual gurus. I realize, of course, that to be critical of what

Oprah says or does is, in the minds of many, to be critical of the divine. Indeed, *USA Today* even ran an article titled: "The divine Miss Winfrey?"

To her credit, Oprah lavishly gives money for many philanthropic causes, and through Angel Network and the Use Your Life Award she has made a difference in the lives of many children. She has funded scholarships for black colleges, written checks to churches, and moved families out of the inner city. More recently she has used her wealth to build a school for disadvantaged children in Africa.

Because Oprah was sexually abused as a child, she is able to empathize with those who suffer—particularly those who have been through the same experience. She has courageously taken on issues such as domestic violence and marital infidelity; she has pulled back the curtain and helped expose the reality of these important issues.

So far, so good.

WHY OPRAH?

Why should we discuss what Oprah believes about Jesus? After all, she does not claim to be a pastor or preacher. She does not have a degree in theology and makes no claim to being a biblical scholar. To her credit, she does not hold herself up as a god; she is just doing what she does, or more accurately, what she feels called to do. She is at the top or near the top of any list of the most admired women in the world. We cannot overstate the connection and impact she has with millions of viewers every day.

Oprah is entitled to her own opinion about Jesus, and whether she's right or wrong, she has to be respected for the good work she does. Yet we cannot ignore her view of Jesus for a couple of compelling reasons.

First, because she is a spiritual leader. The article in *USA Today* says, "After two decades of searching for her authentic self—exploring New Age theories, giving away cars, trotting out fat, recommending good books and tackling countless issues from serious to frivolous—Oprah Winfrey has risen to a new level of guru. . . .

"Over the past year Winfrey has emerged as a spiritual leader for the new millennium, a moral voice of authority for the nation."[1] She has used her pulpit and "has emerged as a symbolic figurehead of spirituality."[2]

If we doubt her impact on her nearly 50 million viewers each week in the United States alone, we can be reminded that a poll on Beliefnet.com reveals that 33 percent of the respondents say that Oprah has had a more profound spiritual impact on them than their clergy. Cathleen Falsani, religion writer for the *Chicago Sun-Times*, asks, "I wonder, has Oprah become America's pastor?"[3]

Claire Zulkey, an Oprah follower who writes about her on an online blog, says, "I think that if this were the equivalent of the Middle Ages and we were to fast-forward 1,200 years, scholars would definitely think that this Oprah person was a deity, if not a canonized being."[4]

Marcia Nelson, whose book *The Gospel according to Oprah* says that it's not going too far to call Oprah a spiritual leader, remarks, "I've said to a number of people—she's today's Billy Graham."[5] Oprah is a woman with a powerful voice, she has a great pulpit, she refers to her show as her "ministry," and she speaks repeatedly of her mission, so we have to evaluate what messages she communicates every day to her vast audience.

The second and most important reason I discuss her in this book is because she is a prototype of most Americans when it comes to belief about Jesus. Oprah's beliefs are a microcosm of the religious landscape of our society. As we shall see, our age is open to Oprah's kind of spirituality but very closed to the unique message about Jesus that the Bible teaches. Ours is a culture in which Jesus is honored but nevertheless consistently slandered.

> Oprah's beliefs are a microcosm of the religious landscape of our society.

Understand that I'm not judging Oprah's personal relationship with God; she has said in an offhand remark that Jesus is her Savior. So where she is in her journey with Jesus is for God to judge. This chapter is not about her as a woman as much as it is about what Darrell Bock calls the "Jesusanity" of our age. Oprah is a window through which we can catch a glimpse into today's spiritually charged pop culture.

WHAT IT TAKES TO PLEASE AN AUDIENCE

What does Oprah teach that is misleading millions? As we shall see, she is teaching people exactly what they want to hear. Could you imagine if she returned to her deeply rooted Baptist background and taught that there is no other way to God except by Jesus? What if she were to say that unless we accept the remedy for our sin offered in Jesus we cannot stand in God's holy presence? Remarks like that would be the demise of her show; millions would switch channels in disgust. The language on the show is permitted to be religious, but not specifically Christian. For example, *Oprah* guests Chip and Jody Ferlaak from Michigan said they were asked to avoid specifically Christian language in relating their story of the devastating accident that killed their four-year-old daughter, Teagan, so that their message of forgiveness would be acceptable to people of different faiths.[6]

"That's understandable," you say. "If she were to stress Christian terminology—especially about Jesus, she would be broadcasting to a very small audience." Exactly. But as we shall see, in making Jesus one option among many, she is slandering Him—and misleading millions.

Oprah, accurately reading what people want to hear, chooses those themes that resonate with our pluralistic, hedonistic, and self-absorbed culture. These messages are finely tuned to the times, and they appeal to the cravings of people who do not see sin as their primary problem. Ours is a culture in which God is not consulted much, and when He is, it's not so much to forgive us, but to help us achieve what we want to become. Let's consider these new age themes and then speak specifically about Jesus.

Spirituality without truth

Spirituality is a big theme in Oprah's telecasts. She says we are essentially spirit beings: "I believe that life is eternal. . . . I believe that it takes on other forms." She told new age guru Gary Zukav, "I am creation's daughter. I am more than my physical self.

I am more than the job I do. I am more than the external definitions that I have given myself. . . . Those are all extensions of who I define myself to be, but ultimately I am Spirit come from the greatest Spirit. I am Spirit."[7]

Oprah, accurately reading what people want to hear, chooses those themes that resonate with our pluralistic, hedonistic, and self-absorbed culture. These messages are finely tuned to the times, and they appeal to the cravings of people who do not see sin as their primary problem.

It is true, of course, that we are spirit, in the sense that we have both a soul and a spirit within our bodies. But when Oprah says, "I am Spirit," she speaks the jargon of the new age movement, which attempts to explore the metaphysical world (the spiritual realm) without a map—that is, without the guidance of the Bible.

Twelve days after September 11, 2001, thousands of people filed into New York City's Yankee Stadium for a religious service to remember the victims and share the survivors' grief with the nation. The program featured an assembled jumble of Christian, Muslim, Jewish, Sikh, and Hindu clergy. The service was profoundly religious, yet utterly pluralistic—and it was hosted by Oprah Winfrey.

"When you lose a loved one, you gain an angel whose name you know," she said. "Over six thousand, and counting, angels [were] added to the spiritual roster these past two weeks. It is my prayer that they will keep us in their sight with a direct line to our hearts."[8] But wait—how does Oprah know that human beings turn into angels after death? Intuition? Wishful thinking? Perhaps we should not be too critical of such statements and simply pass them off as the throwaway lines of a feel-good religion.

But more ominously, when Oprah Winfrey's movie *Beloved* was released, she reported that she had "channeled" some of the historical characters that were being portrayed in the movie. In an interview with movie critic Roger Ebert, Oprah showed him what helped her get ready for the day's filming: actual bills of sale from slave auctions. "Before some scenes," Oprah said, "I would light candles and say their names. . . . I would try to call them in. Call them in with a sense of reverence, because I always thought that this was bigger than my own little self."

Oprah continues. "The first meeting I had with [director] Jonathan Demme, he was concerned about how I was going to lose the Oprah persona, was going to play the character. And I said I didn't know if it could be acted as much as channeled. I felt like I had to open up and receive, as opposed to trying to go in and find."[9]

Yes, mysticism with its attendant spirituality is attractive, and millions are trying to connect with the metaphysical realm for boosts of energy and help in overcoming obstacles. It is a world filled with self-realization, spirit guides, and yes, even miracles. In local libraries, shelves are stacked with books on miracles, psychic energy, and the mind sciences. Hundreds of Web sites are devoted to these themes.

But the Bible warns against all forms of occultism, whether it is channeling spirits, imitation miracles, or astrology. The Scriptures teach that two spirit realms occupy the same atmosphere in which we live: the realm of God and His good angels, and the realm of Satan and his evil angels. And since the dark side of the spirit world attempts to imitate God, we should not be surprised that people are often deceived, mistaking satanic "demons of light" for contact with the living God. Be assured that Oprah was not in contact with dead slaves or heaven-sent entities; the dark side of the spirit world is always available and willing to connect with gullible humans.

Spirituality without truth leads to dazzling deceptions. Only the Bible can give us the discernment we need in this pluralistic age.

Psychology without theology

Oprah promotes a psychology that is, for the most part, the gospel of self-fulfillment. Cut off from rigorous doctrinal understanding, this psychology is self-focused. The mantra is this: Do what meets your needs and what gives you fulfillment; *look out for number one!* And how do you achieve this ideal fulfillment? Make much of yourself and hope that others will make much of you as well.

In teaching psychology without theology, Oprah has become what someone called "a high priestess and icon of the psychoization of American society." When she features new age gurus on her show, she makes new age ideas seem mainstream to her millions of viewers worldwide. As one person says, "Oprah's clothes may bear labels, but her faith does not."[10]

According to new age thought, if I want to have a good self-image, I need affirmation; I need to feel good about myself, whether I should feel good about myself or not. *I* am the center of my world, *I* deserve to be happy, and *I* have the responsibility of making myself happy. I might be sleeping with my neighbor's spouse, but I should feel good about myself, managing my relationships as best I can.

But personal fulfillment cannot be found without a commitment to the hard principles of fidelity and God-honoring integrity. The worship of self excludes the worship of God. John Piper writes, "Our fatal error is believing that wanting to be happy means wanting to be made much of. It feels so good to be affirmed. But the good feeling is finally rooted in the worth of self, not the worth of God. This path to happiness is an illusion."

Piper goes on to say that no one goes to the Grand Canyon to increase his self-esteem; this is a reminder, he says, that "soul-health and great happiness come not from beholding a great self but a great splendor."[11] Oprah is speaking into a culture that is so self-absorbed it cannot even imagine that the real secret of happiness is to adore someone other than ourselves. Yet it is in the adoration of and submission to God that we find the true pathway to happiness. Hear it from the lips of Jesus: "Blessed are the pure in heart, for they will see God" (Matthew 5:8). And as Augustine famously wrote, "O God, thou has made us for thyself and our hearts are restless until they have found their all in thee."

Psychology without theology creates a man-centered absorption that feeds our egos and either neglects or belittles God. Al Mohler writes, "Oprah's newly-packaged positive-thinking spirituality is tailor-made for the empty souls of our postmodern age. She promises meaning without truth, acceptance without judgment, and fulfillment without self-denial."[12]

The gospel that entertains is a gospel that cannot redeem.

WHY NOT ONE WAY AMONG MANY?

And now we come to the heart of Oprah's most misleading teaching, which blends in nicely with the lifestyle of self-absorption and personal excess. I shall summarize a panel discussion Oprah offered on the topic of spirituality, Jesus, and the force called God. Follow this carefully.

> Oprah is speaking into a culture that is so self-absorbed it cannot even imagine that the real secret of happiness is to adore someone other than ourselves.

One member of the discussion—evidently arguing for Christianity—says there are two forces in the world, God and the power of darkness.

Oprah asks whether we can choose between the two and the panel member says, "Absolutely."

Oprah then says that one of the mistakes we make is to believe there is only one way to live, even though there are "diverse ways of being in the world."

The panel member asks, "How do you please God?"

Oprah answers, "There are many ways, many paths to what you call God." Gesturing to another panel member, she continues, "And her path might be something else when she gets there and she might call it the light but her loving and her kindness and her generosity brings her—if it brings her to the same point that it brings you, it doesn't matter if she calls it God along the way or not."

The panel member responds that there is only one way to God, but Oprah argues that there could not possibly be only one way.

The discussion progresses and then Oprah asks this provocative question: *"Does God care about your heart or does God care about if you call His Son Jesus?"*[13]

This is a critical question. What she is asking is this: Is it possible to have your heart right before God even if you don't accept Jesus as the only path to God? And given the context of the question and Oprah's other comments about Jesus, it is quite clear that she expects a particular answer. In other words, if we are good people—if our hearts are right—it doesn't matter whether we call God's Son Jesus. Any other path would do. As long as our hearts are right, the content of our faith does not matter very much.

Oprah represents the whole new age characterization of Jesus, presenting Him as a wonderful role model, a prophet, and a teacher—and maybe even a Savior. But if He is a Savior, He is one among many. He might be *my* Savior, but He does not have to be *your* Savior. He is not the Lord of lords, but a lord among other lords. He is the optional, no-obligation Jesus.

The bottom line, following this line of reasoning, is that we can all approach God on our own, as long as we have the right attitude of heart. God cares about whether we are good people, not whether we are rightly related to Jesus. It is the quality of our lives, not the content of our beliefs, that matters to God.

Here at last, the core issue of the Christian faith is exposed: Are there diverse paths to the divine, or is Jesus the only way?

And would it not be bigotry to say that Jesus is the only way to the Father? Why can't we say that God is more interested in our hearts than He is in our beliefs?

In the following pages I will show why there are not and cannot be diverse paths to the divine. For reasons that will become clear, all other gurus and prophets fall short of the qualifications needed to be a Savior. There are compelling reasons why there is only one mediator between God and man.

Jesus is the only way because:

The nature of sin demands it

I begin with the doctrine of sin because it lies at the heart of the discussion about whether or not Jesus is one among many different ways to God. If sin is defined out of existence—if the only sin of our culture is eating chocolate, then one religion is as good as another. But the more seriously we take sin, the more desperately we need a Savior.

Our culture says there are many ways to God because we have lost our capacity to despise our sin. The modern mind does not encourage moral reproach, and it especially does not encourage self-reproach. Cornelius Plantinga Jr. points out that today pride is no longer viewed with alarm, but rather is praised and cultivated. Our list of virtues and vices, he says, has shrunk to include only two: tolerance and intolerance.[14] To be sure, people are still willing to make moral judgments, but only on those who make moral judgments. They say things like "It is always wrong to make moral judgments."[15]

The Bible describes us in our natural state as sinners both by nature and by choice. And our conscience agrees. In our quiet moments we all know that we are sinful—thoroughly sinful. Just recently I sat next to a man on an airplane who told me that he thinks he can make it into heaven his own way, based upon his own merits. I asked him if his merits included even his thoughts—and then I asked him what would happen if his thoughts were shown on a JumboTron for all of his colleagues and church friends to see. He said he would prefer to live on a private island! And so would I!

Frankly, we are unable to assess the true state of our souls. We are obsessed with self-protection and self-aggrandizement, very capable of seeing the sins of others but quite blinded by our own. We're like the boy who told his mother he was ten feet tall, and he was—according to the yardstick he had made.

Sin is a deadly burden to the soul. Left to ourselves we are really lost, unable to deliver ourselves from the curse. Christians do not measure sin by comparing one person with another, or by how good we might feel about ourselves. *Christians measure the seriousness of sin by the suffering needed to atone for it.*

More on that in a moment.

The holiness of God demands it

What we believe about God, said A. W. Tozer, is the most important thing about us. So, I must ask, what do you believe about God?

If we believe that the Almighty is just a higher version of ourselves, then we will not be seriously concerned about our sin. We will tell ourselves that we are quite fine, thank you very much. But if we accept the God of the Bible, whose searing holiness and justice must be satisfied in order for us to stand in His presence, then we will know that we need divine intervention in order to be saved from the wrath to come.

Let's look at two important warnings recorded in the Bible. The first commandment stipulates that we must come before the right God: "You shall have no other gods before me" (Exodus 20:3). In other words, we cannot remake God to be someone or something agreeable to our own desires and aptitudes.

The second warning is that we must approach the right God in the right way. Early on, Cain and Abel represented two different ways of approaching God. Abel brought the right sacrifice accompanied by faith, but his brother brought his own sacrifice accompanied by an attitude of self-righteous entitlement. You know the rest of the story: Cain murdered Abel because he was jealous of his brother's acceptance by God. Both came to the right God, but only one came in the right way. *God has the right to prescribe the way we should come to Him.*

Our greatest temptation is to create a God just like us: forgiving, inclusive, and endlessly tolerant. We are tempted to think that because we are quick to excuse ourselves, that God is also very forgiving, no matter what we do or believe. As long as we "do the best we can" with the cards we have been dealt, "He will accept us." We are notori-

> If we accept the God of the Bible, whose searing holiness and justice must be satisfied in order for us to stand in His presence, then we will know that we need divine intervention in order to be saved from the wrath to come.

ous for suppressing the truth we dislike. We really don't care if we grieve God.

But God—the God of the Bible—is impeccably just. He cannot allow bygones to be bygones. Sin is a personal affront to this personal God, and all sin must be accounted for. There must be satisfaction before reconciliation takes place. To put it frankly but biblically, the wrath of God over our sin must be averted, and someone must take our place—someone who can bear the burden of God's righteous anger against sin, someone qualified to give us the righteousness that God accepts. Donald McCullough writes:

> One may appear before other gods with a sense of confidence, with no sense of being threatened. They will stay put; they won't stray from the places assigned to them by human egos desperately trying to remain in control. But the God revealed in Jesus Christ is holy, and a holy God cannot be contained or tamed.[16]

All other religions fall short in their understanding of God and therefore cannot understand the seriousness of sin. Because they have no remedy for sin they treat it lightly, urging us to do better and try to improve our behavior. When faced with criminals who have destroyed themselves and others, other religions have little to say except perhaps to talk about God's mercy. But when pressed, they admit they have no valid reason to suppose that God will actually forgive us, so they offer only a faint hope of acceptance and reconciliation.

When a university professor converted to Christianity, her colleagues asked her, "Why Christianity? Why not Buddhism or Hinduism?" She candidly answered, "No other religion has a solution for my sin." And that is true. Buddha did not claim to be a Savior, nor did Krishna or Mohammed, who said he was not even sure of his own eternal salvation.

The more we attempt to remove our sin on our own, the more persistent its power and deception. We are in critical need of intervention by a Savior with the qualifications to save us.

The sacrifice of Jesus demands it

How perfect do you have to be in order for God to accept you? Ask the average person and he might say something like "Well, not too perfect, because God is forgiving." Yes, God is forgiving, but the biblical answer is this: *You must be as perfect as God, and if you aren't, don't even think you will be welcomed into God's heaven!*

> How perfect do you have to be in order for God to accept you?

Of course it must be so. The holiness of God is unbending, never fading, and ever demanding. In fact, the only holiness God accepts is His own. Our goodness, whatever it might be, always falls woefully short of what God demands. "All have sinned and fall short of the glory of God" (Romans 3:23). The glory of God, not our perceived goodness, is the divine standard.

Let me explain. If we have to be as perfect as God for Him to accept us, we have an obvious problem! Clearly, there is a sharp distinction between our goodness and God's absolute goodness, the goodness (or holiness) that is an essential part of who He is. There is an infinite chasm between Him and us. So how is this gap to be bridged? We need a kind of righteousness of which we have none!

The only one qualified to do this for us is Jesus. As a man He represents us to God, but as God (the second Person of the Trinity), He can give us what God requires. The Bible promises that through faith in the sacrifice Jesus made on the cross, we are credited with His righteousness. So thanks to Him, we can stand in God's presence and *be welcomed as if we were Jesus!*

Put all this together: God's nature demands that sin must be paid for, either by the sinner or someone who stands in his or her stead. Our own sin is so serious that if we have to pay for it ourselves, we will be suffering eternally in hell. But Jesus, the second Person of the Trinity, came to die in our place and suffered our eternal penalty in His six hours on the cross. Now He not only takes away our sin but gives us His righteousness—the very righteousness we need for God to receive us. If you've followed this so far you know that God demands perfect holiness from us and in Jesus *God supplies what He demands!*

There is a story about a judge who demanded two hundred dollars from a defendant who did not have any money. So the judge left the bench, took off his robe, and stood beside the defendant; then he took money out of his own pocket and laid it on the table. The judge donned his robe again, sat down at his desk, and reached over to take the money he had placed on the table. Then he said to the surprised defendant, "You may leave, since your fine has been paid!"

Just so, Jesus left heaven and stood beside us, paying a debt we could not pay, and now we have this promise: "Yet to all who received him, to those who believed in his name, he gave the right to become children of God" (John 1:12).

Do you now understand why there cannot be diverse paths to God? Only God can supply what He demands; only Jesus has the credentials to be a Savior. Gurus and prophets are many, but there is only one Savior who can bridge the gap between God and us and do it entirely on God's terms!

We cannot mediate our own relationship with God; God has to supply His own mediator to bring us together. This mediator, Jesus, is one of us in that He was human, but He is also one with God because He is divine.

> Only God can supply what He demands; only Jesus has the credentials to be a Savior. Gurus and prophets are many, but there is only one Savior who can bridge the gap between God and us and do it entirely on God's terms!

Think of how remarkable this is. In the Old Testament, priests brought sacrifices on behalf of the people. The priests stood in need of a sacrifice just as much as the people they represented. But when Jesus came to redeem us, as our Priest He also became our sacrifice! He did not sacrifice a lamb, but He sacrificed Himself on our behalf. A sacrifice, if it is to be effective, must be equal to the sins committed. And since sin is against an infinite being, so the sacrifice—in this case, Jesus—must have infinite value. Christianity affirms that Jesus suffered terribly, because sin is terrible.

If we ask why God accepts only Jesus, the answer is that the very nature of God demands it. Only Jesus can lift our curse and confidently bring us into God's presence.

In a condemned world, we are not in a position to find our own way to God, and we should be grateful that there is a way at all—even if there is only one. The reason we think there are many ways to God is that we have lost our capacity to despise our sin. And resistance to redemption counts as sin too, often displaying a special perversity.[17]

BACK TO OPRAH'S QUESTION

Let's return to Oprah's question: Is God more interested in our hearts or in His demand that we call His Son Jesus? The answer is this: God is interested in our hearts—indeed that is the focus of His attention, but we cannot have a clean heart *unless* we call His Son Jesus.

Self-salvation doesn't work for sinners. If you try to wash a dirty well with water from the same well, it will never get clean. To think that we, by our own efforts, are able to cleanse our hearts is folly indeed. Some people have been known to confess their sins on national television with the hope that the experience will be a catharsis, a cleansing of the heart because all the failures of the past are put out there for all to see. But confession to other human beings does not cleanse the heart, for that is a work that only God can do. Already in the Old Testament, God says, "I will sprinkle clean water on you, and you will be clean; I will cleanse you from all your impurities and from all your idols. I will give you a new heart and put a new spirit in you" (Ezekiel 36:25-26).

133

In the New Testament, we are promised that the sacrifice of Jesus can "cleanse our consciences from acts that lead to death, so that we may serve the living God" (Hebrews 9:14). Left to ourselves, we can have a heart that does good things, but we cannot have a heart that is made clean and that loves God more than self.

As a woman once told me, "I cannot take steel wool to my heart to scrub it!" No, she can't and neither can we. She needs a forgiving God to enter deep within her psyche and cleanse her within. Thankfully, she accepted God's Son to do it.

If you have never received Christ as Savior and Redeemer, this would be a good opportunity to do so.

Father,
I thank You that Jesus died on the cross
so that I could be forgiven and received by You.
Today I receive Him as my sin bearer;
I accept that He died in my place.
I pray not only that my sins would be forgiven
but that You might cleanse my heart and give me
new desires for You and for holiness.
As best as I know how,
I entrust myself to You
for now and eternity.
Amen.

Finding a Jesus You Can Trust

"Exposing the Greatest Cover-Up in History"

That's the subtitle of Michael Baigent's book *The Jesus Papers*, which purports to be a retelling of the early days of Christianity. Specifically, Baigent believes that Jesus was married to Mary Magdalene, escaped the Crucifixion, and spent His remaining days in a monastery in Egypt. Like *The Da Vinci Code*, this book is largely fiction, but the difference is that Baigent passes his book off as if it were sober history. It begins its flight from reality in the early pages and carries on a lengthy imaginative scenario all the way to the end.

The Jesus Papers refer to two papyrus letters that were discovered when a man was digging a cellar near the Temple area in Jerusalem. The author of these letters claims to be the Messiah of the children of Israel. He explains that he is not God but that the spirit of God is within him, and "everyone who felt similarly filled with the 'spirit' was also a 'son of God.'"[1]

Although Baigent talked the owner into showing him the letters, he was unable to decipher them, since he was unacquainted with Aramaic. And even though no other scholar has seen the papers or translated them, Baigent is convinced that these papers, if translated, would destroy historic Christianity.

So there you have it: An untranslated manuscript to which no scholars have access will someday shake the world and disprove everything we know about Jesus! Apparently this document does not have to be held up to serious historical scrutiny, because Baigent seems to know in advance that it will be more trustworthy than the traditional sources. I am reminded of Winston Churchill, who is quoted as saying that the desire to believe something often outweighs rationality and evidence.

This is a clear example of the way many scholars today are willing to give marginal (or worse) evidence, such as the Gnostic Gospels, priority over the primary sources of Matthew, Mark, Luke, and John. Imagine applying this principle to other areas of life: Suppose a crime is committed and you have four eyewitnesses who essentially tell the same story. Even under cross-examination, they all agree. But you are unhappy with their conclusions and you want to disprove their claims. So you interview people who weren't eyewitnesses but were born years after the crime was committed. Then on the basis of *their* testimony, you spin theories about what *might* have happened; you jump from what *could* have happened to the supposition that it *did* in fact happen, and soon you have an entirely different scenario. Then you hype this idea as a previously suppressed story of what *really* happened.

Having chosen to cut yourself off from the primary sources, you now can rewrite history according to your preference and liking. Of course, you use the primary sources if they happen to agree with you and discount them when they contradict your theory. Better to believe an untranslated, inaccessible manuscript than documents that have been scrutinized for centuries.

The logic is inescapable: If it walks like a duck, quacks like a duck, and lays duck eggs, it obviously must be *a camel*!

THE FACTS AS THEY ARE

Like it or not, the best witnesses we have to the early days of the Christian church are the manuscripts of the New Testament. These documents have been analyzed, marginalized, and vilified by those who are adverse to miracles and the claims of Jesus, and yet there they are, open to examination of the most rigorous kind.

There are compelling reasons why a wedge cannot be driven between the Jesus of the Gospels and the Jesus of history. There is indeed a rope—not a string, but a rope with many strands— that leads us from the early beginnings of the Christian church right back to Jesus as He is portrayed in the Gospels. The Gospels are interwoven with the events of secular history in such a way that if you believe the one, you have good reason to believe the other.

Let's spend a moment in historical reflection.

First, consider that the life and times of Jesus were contemporaneous with several other religious and political personages: John the Baptist, Tiberius Caesar, Pilate, Herod (Antipas), and the high priesthood of Annas and Caiaphas. What makes this significant is that we have detailed knowledge of these people in secular literature. By studying the interaction that Jesus had with these people, we learn first that we are able to locate the ministry and movements of Jesus firmly within the historical context of Galilee, and second that we are able to verify the reliability of

139

the Gospel accounts by showing how they fit into the secular references of the day.

From secular sources we learn these facts: Jesus lived during the time of Tiberius Caesar; He was a wonder-worker, He had a brother named James, He was acclaimed to be the Messiah, and He was crucified under Pontius Pilate. In fact, we also learn that He was crucified on the eve of the Jewish Passover and that darkness and an earthquake occurred when He died. His disciples believed that He rose from the dead, and they were willing to die for their belief. Denying Roman gods, they worshiped Jesus as God.[2] This is compelling evidence that the Gospels of the New Testament are consistent with the historical context given to us by non-Christian writers.

Consider also that the writings of Paul, which are among the earliest books of the New Testament to be written, assume that the churches would know the various teachings about Jesus. In other words, although the Epistles might have been written before the Gospels (1 Corinthians, for example, was written in about AD 52, whereas most scholars believe that Matthew was written a few years later), these Epistles presuppose

> There are compelling reasons why a wedge cannot be driven between the Jesus of the Gospels and the Jesus of history. There is indeed a rope—not a string, but a rope with many strands— that leads us from the early beginnings of the Christian church right back to Jesus as He is portrayed in the Gospels.

the teachings of Jesus as later recorded in the Gospels. Contrary to popular speculation, there is no way that Paul could have changed the doctrines of the early church and then expected the early Christians to believe his writings. They believed what he wrote because what he taught was consistent with what they already knew.

Second, it strains credulity to accept the notion that the early apostles knew the historical Jesus as a mere man and then later chose to deify Him and proclaim Him as the unique Son of God who performed miracles and rose from the dead. When Peter stood up on the day of Pentecost, he proclaimed the same Jesus he and the other disciples had come to know as followers. He was not embellishing the story out of a sincere desire to find someone in whom he could believe. In a thoughtful message worthy of careful analysis, he said,

> Men of Israel, listen to this: Jesus of Nazareth was a man accredited by God to you by miracles, wonders and signs, which God did among you through him, *as you yourselves know*. . . .God raised him from the dead, freeing him from the agony of death, because it was impossible for death to keep its hold on him. . . . God has raised this Jesus to life, and *we are all witnesses* of the fact. Exalted to the right hand of God, he has received from the Father the promised Holy Spirit and has poured out what you now see and hear.
> ACTS 2:22, 24, 32-33 (emphasis mine)

The point cannot be made too strongly: The Jesus of history and the Christ of faith are one and the same person! Peter was not making up some new theory about who Jesus was, but was simply proclaiming the Christ he knew to an audience that was very much aware of the miracles Jesus had done among them. To deify a man was the highest blasphemy (Exodus 20:3), but Jesus proved to skeptics that He was worthy to be worshipped as both Lord and Christ.

The Jesus of history and the Christ of faith are one and the same person!

The origins of Christianity are not mythical, rooted in the shimmering hope that a mere man could be made into a god. The Jesus proclaimed by the early church is the same Jesus who was born in Bethlehem, walked this earth, and died and rose again in the city of Jerusalem. He is the same Jesus whose words and deeds convinced His followers that He was the long-awaited Messiah.

THE TIME GAP

The objection is often made that there was a lengthy time gap between Jesus' ministry and the writing of the Gospels. If Jesus was crucified in AD 33, and the Gospels were written twenty-five or thirty years later, is it not possible that radical changes were made between what Jesus actually did and said and what was later recorded? Couldn't the accounts have been embellished? And if not, what did the believers do during that long period of time when there were no written records and when many who knew Jesus were dying off?

The answer to these questions is to understand the religious culture of the day. It was customary at that time for rabbis to carefully hand over their teachings to their disciples, who held tightly to what was said. These disciples in turn handed these same teachings to the next generation of disciples, and so on. Great care was taken to deliver the exact wording that had been handed down. Rabbi Eliezer ben Hyrcanus declared, "I have never said in my life a thing that I did not hear from my teachers."[3] Indeed, it was said that whoever forgot a word of the Scripture that had been handed over should account it as if he had lost his soul.

Jesus often couched His teachings in memorable forms such as aphorisms, rhyme, poetry, and parallelism. This enabled them to be preserved intact. Certainly it is also possible that the followers of Jesus had written records of His teachings before the four Gospels were written. Such a collection could have been disseminated in the early churches and then included in the Gospels in their final form.[4] Indeed, in his preface, Luke says that he based his Gospel on eyewitnesses and other written accounts (Luke 1:1-3).

Whereas the typical rabbi had one pupil, Jesus chose twelve. And since no rabbi was as important to Judaism as Jesus was to Christianity, particular care would have been given to His words and actions. Jesus was careful to train His students to go into the world to bear *His* message and not their own. They formulated various summaries of His life and teaching that they would repeat as they spread the Word.

THE RABBI WHO SPOKE FOR HIMSELF

Jesus was very different from the rabbis of His day, who were careful to recite only what they were taught—often mingled with centuries of misleading interpretations and traditions. But Jesus spoke for Himself. With an authority that set His hearers on edge, He would say, "You have heard that it was said . . . but I tell you . . ."

The Pharisees who heard Jesus' teachings could not believe their ears. A man who was perhaps thirty years old was claiming to be the Messiah and promising that those who believed in Him would have eternal life. These seemed like the words of a lunatic. John 8 gives us an interesting look at their reaction to Jesus.

> The Jews answered him, "Aren't we right in saying that you are a Samaritan and demon-possessed?"
>
> "I am not possessed by a demon," said Jesus, "but I honor my Father and you dishonor me. I am not seeking glory for myself; but there is one who seeks it, and he is the judge. I tell you the truth, if anyone keeps my word, he will never see death."
>
> At this the Jews exclaimed, "Now we know that you are demon-possessed! Abraham died and so did the prophets, yet you say that if anyone keeps your word, he will never taste death. Are you greater than our father Abraham? He died, and so did the prophets. Who do you think you are?"
>
> Jesus replied, "If I glorify myself, my glory means nothing. My Father, whom you claim as your God, is the one who glorifies me. Though you do not know him, I know him. If I said I did not, I would be a liar like you, but I do know

him and keep his word. Your father Abraham rejoiced at
the thought of seeing my day; he saw it and was glad."

"You are not yet fifty years old," the Jews said to him, "and
you have seen Abraham!"

"I tell you the truth," Jesus answered, "before Abraham was
born, I am!"   JOHN 8:48-58

The Jews knew that Jesus had often claimed to be God.
Now even the incredulous realized that His words could be
interpreted in no other way. He had identified Himself with the
"I AM," Jehovah who appeared to Moses in the burning bush
(Exodus 3:14).

Now, if He wasn't God but instead only a man, this was the
highest form of blasphemy. So the Jews did what they should
have done with blasphemers—they gathered stones to stone
Him. Little wonder Jesus caused such a stir!

And what shall we make of this statement from Jesus: "For
just as the Father raises the dead and gives them life, even so
the Son gives life to whom he is pleased to give it. Moreover,
the Father judges no one, but has entrusted all judgment to the
Son, that all may honor the Son just as they honor the Father.
He who does not honor the Son does not honor the Father, who
sent him" (John 5:21-23)?

Day after day, Jesus spoke words that only God could speak
and did works that only God could do. A prophet might do a
few miracles, but only God can forgive sin. Only God can judge
human beings after death. Jesus did not claim to be a god in

some lesser sense; He claimed to be Jehovah, the omnipotent and omnipresent God of the Old Testament.

The deity of Jesus rends a clean and unbridgeable chasm between Christianity and other religious options. And for this reason, it also means that other religions cannot logically claim Jesus as one of a long line of prophets. Since He claimed to be God, it follows that He would assert exclusivity. After Jesus told the disciples that He was going away, Thomas asked Him a question: "Lord, we don't know where you are going, so how can we know the way?" (John 14:5).

Christ's response was to the point: "I am the way and the truth and the life. No one comes to the Father except through me" (John 14:6).

All attempts to reinterpret this verse to blunt its meaning have been contrived; they fail because the words are so clear, so consistent with the rest of Christ's teachings.

Our world is filled with guides who claim to know something the rest of us don't. Hundreds of false teachers have gathered a following, but in the end they have been shown to be just as fallible as those who follow them. Death proves them to be as vulnerable as the rest of us to the limitations of humanity.

When Jesus said "No one comes to the Father except through me," He narrowed the gate, He built a fence along the road, and He pointed to where the path led. We have no right to try to tear down the gateposts, make the road broader, or choose a destination according to our own liking. All other paths lead somewhere else; they go away from the Father, not toward Him.

Jesus taught that there were two paths: an attractive broad way that led to destruction and the narrow way that often was overlooked. "Enter through the narrow gate. For wide is the gate and broad is the road that leads to destruction, and many enter through it. But small is the gate and narrow the road that leads to life, and only a few find it" (Matthew 7:13-14). The broad way is deceptive because many so-called enlightened religious leaders have labeled it the way to life. Jesus confronts us with two paths, two separate gates, and two separate destinations.

> The deity of Jesus rends a clean and unbridgeable chasm between Christianity and other religious options.

To quote Stephen Neill, "[Christian faith] maintains that in Jesus the one thing that needed to happen has happened in such a way that it need never happen again in the same way. . . . The bridge has been built. There is room on it for all the needed traffic in both directions, from God to man and from man to God. Why look for any other?"[5]

Today people speak about moving beyond Christianity to something better. New Agers say that Christianity is like a boat that is necessary to take you across the river, but once you disembark you are free to transcend it and enter into a whole new existence. Christianity is like baby steps, but then we must move on to something more mystical, satisfying, or complete. But as I once heard someone say, to move beyond love is to lust, to move beyond rationality is to go insane, and to move beyond medicine is to drink poison. And to move beyond Christianity is to believe in error and gross deception. Christ is the one Man you can never move beyond without falling into a deep pit.

Strictly speaking, it is not possible to move beyond Christianity; we must abandon Christianity if we want to move beyond it! Whenever we try to add to Christianity, we subtract from it. Just as wine is diluted with every drop of water, so the power of the gospel must remain distinct or be reduced to something it was never meant to be. Those who surrender the uniqueness of Christ do not simply surrender a part of the Christian message, they surrender it entirely. We cannot remove the foundation and profess that the building is still intact.

A CONTRAST OF CLAIMS

During the Russian revolution of 1918, Lenin said that if Communism were implemented, there would be bread for every household. Yet he never had the nerve to say, "I am the bread of life. He who comes to me will never go hungry, and he who believes in me will never be thirsty" (John 6:35).

> Those who surrender the uniqueness of Christ do not simply surrender a part of the Christian message, they surrender it entirely.

Hitler made astounding claims for the role of Germany on this planet, believing that he was beginning a thousand-year Reich (rule). Despite these outlandish claims, he never said, "I tell you the truth, whoever hears my word and believes him who sent me has eternal life and will not be condemned; he has crossed over from death to life" (John 5:24).

Buddha taught enlightenment, yet he died seeking more light. He never said, "I am the light of the world. Whoever follows me will never walk in darkness, but will have the light of life" (John 8:12).

Mohammed claimed that he and his tribes were descendants from Abraham through Ishmael, one of Abraham's sons. But he did not say, "Before Abraham was born, I am!" (John 8:58).

Freud believed that psychotherapy would heal people's emotional and spiritual pains. But he could not say, "Peace I leave with you; my peace I give you. I do not give to you as the world gives. Do not let your hearts be troubled and do not be afraid" (John 14:27).

New age gurus say that we will all be reincarnated, yet not a one of them can say, "I am the resurrection and the life. He who believes in me will live, even though he dies; and whoever lives and believes in me will never die" (John 11:25-26).

At a Bible study I met a Jewish woman, Adriane Millman, who related how desperately she had prayed every day that she would find the truth about how to have a personal relationship with God. The very thought that Jesus might indeed be the Son of God, the Messiah, frightened her. *Oh God,* she often prayed, *please be anyone but Jesus!*

But at the end of her search, she said, her worst fear came to pass—God turned out to be Jesus! There are some good reasons to believe that she is right. Since Christianity makes the astounding claim that "God was in Christ reconciling the world to Himself" (2 Corinthians 5:19, NKJV), I urge you to face the question: *Who, then, is Jesus?* Is He a liar? a lunatic? a legend?

Or is He Lord? Jesus simply does not allow us the luxury of neutrality. If you have never accepted this Jesus as your Savior, do it now; to do any less is to slander Him.

> Father, I thank You that You sent Jesus to die for my sins.
> I confess Him to be Savior and Lord. I now accept Him as my personal sin bearer. At this moment I receive the free offer of eternal life Jesus gave to all who believe. As best I can, I give myself to You and thank You that I can belong to You forever.

> Amen.

Endnotes

From the Pen of an Atheist

1. Sam Harris, *Letter to a Christian Nation* (New York: Alfred A. Knopf, 2006), 3–4.

2. Harris, *Letter to a Christian Nation*, 5.

Jesus in the Spin Zone

1. Joseph Smith, "Revelation? Part 3—Plundering History," Sydney Anglicans Network (29 August 2006), http://your.sydneyanglicans.net/indepth/articles/plundering_ history, last accessed 4/18/2007.

2. Joseph Stowell, *The Trouble With Jesus* (Chicago: Moody Press, 2003), 77–78.

3. This quote was made by Darrell Bock during a lecture on Jesus at Beason School of Theology, July 28, 2006.

4. Robert W. Funk, Roy W. Hoover, and the Jesus Seminar, *The Five Gospels: What Did Jesus Really Say?* (New York: Scribner, 1993), 2.

5. Jerry Adler, "In Search of the Spiritual," *Newsweek,* September 2005, 49.

Lie #1: Jesus' Family Tomb Has Been Discovered

1. Craig Evans, "The Jesus Tomb Show—Bibical Archaeologists Reject Discovery Channel Show's Claims," http://craigaevans.com/tombofjesus.htm, last accessed 4/18/2007.

2. Ibid.

3. James Cameron, introduction to *The Jesus Family Tomb—the Discovery, the Investigation, and the Evidence That Could Change History,* Simcha Jacobovici and Charles Pellegrino (San Francisco: HarperSanFrancisco, 2007), x.

4. Jacobovici and Pellegrino, *The Jesus Family Tomb,* 71.

5. Cameron, introduction to *The Jesus Family Tomb,* vii.

6. Ibid., xiii.

7. Jacobovici and Pellegrino, *The Jesus Family Tomb*, 75

8. Craig Evans, "The Jesus Tomb Show."

9. Craig Evans, "The Jesus Tomb Show."

10. Ibid.

11. Christopher Mims, "Has James Cameron Found Jesus's Tomb or Is It Just a Statistical Error?" *Scientific American*, 2 March 2007.

12. Ibid.

13. Craig Evans, "The Jesus Tomb Show."

Lie #2: Jesus Was Not Crucified

1. Chawkat Moucarry, *The Prophet and the Messiah—An Arab Christian's Perspective on Islam and Christianity* (Downers Grove: InterVarsity Press, 2001), 127. This is an excellent book for those who want a more thorough understanding of Jesus' role in Islamic teaching.

2. Ibid., 135.

3. Norman Geisler and Abdul Saleeb, *Answering Islam* (Grand Rapids: Baker Books, 1993), 67.

4. Moucarry, *The Prophet and the Messiah*, 156.

5. Peter Jones, *The Gnostic Empire Strikes Back* (Phillipsburg, NJ: P&R Publishing, 1992), 25.

6. Mark Durie, *Revelation? Do We Worship the Same God?* (Upper Mt. Gravatt, Australia: CityHarvest Publications, 2006), 39, 47.

7. Moucarry, *The Prophet and the Messiah*, 140.

8. Ibid., 139.

9. Geisler and Saleeb, *Answering Islam*, 207–226.

10. Ibid., 230.

11. Ibid.

12. Moucarry, *The Prophet and the Messiah*, 157.

13. Ibid., 158.

14. John Piper, *The Passion of Jesus Christ* (Wheaton: Crossway Books, 2004), 21.

15. Ibid., 20.

16. Moucarry, *The Prophet and the Messiah*, 161.

17. John Ankerberg and Dillon Burroughs, *Middle East Meltdown* (Eugene, OR: Harvest House Publishers, 2007), 33.

18. *Washington Post*, 20 February 2002.

19. Edward Shillito, "Jesus of the Scars," *Areopagus Proclamation* 10, no.7 (April 2000).

20. See Durie, *Revelation?*, 25; Moucarry, *The Prophet and the Messiah*, 139.

Lie #3: Judas Did Jesus a Favor

1. Dante Alighieri, *The Inferno*, Canto XXXIV. Brutus and Cassius also reside in the deepest recesses, presumably for their treachery and suicide.

2. William Klassen, *Judas: Betrayer or Friend of Jesus?* (Minneapolis: Fortress Press, 1996).

3. James M. Robinson, *The Secrets of Judas* (San Francisco: HarperSanFrancisco, 2006).

4. E. J. Dionne Jr., "A New Twist on Judas: Beyond the Buzz Over Gospel's Publication," *Washington Post*, 14 April 2006.

5. Rodolphe Kasser, Marvin Meyer, and Gregor Wurst, eds., *The Gospel of Judas* (Washington: National Geographic Society, 2006), 19.

6. Ibid., 20.

7. Ibid., 20–21.

8. Ibid., 32–33.

9. Ibid., 33.

10. Ibid., 31.

11. Ibid., 42.

12. This, of course, is the ancient heresy called *Docetism.*

13. Kasser, Meyer, and Wurst, eds., *The Gospel of Judas,* 43.

14. N. T. Wright, *Judas and the Gospel of Jesus: Have We Missed the Truth about Christianity?* (Grand Rapids: Baker Books, 2006).

15. Gregor Wurst, "Irenaeus of Lyon and the Gospel of Judas," in *The Gospel of Judas,* 123.

16. James M. Robinson, *The Secrets of Judas* (San Francisco: HarperSanFrancico, 2006), vii.

17. Ibid.

18. *The Passion Play 2000: Oberammergau* (Germany: The Gemeinde Oberammergau, 2000), 71.

Lie #4: Jesus Was Only a Man

1. Erik Reece, "Jesus Without the Miracles—Thomas Jefferson's Bible and the Gospel of Thomas," *Harper's*, December 2005, 33.

2. Ibid., 24.

3. Stephen Mitchell, as quoted by David Van Biema, "The Gospel Truth?" *Time*, 8 April 1996.

4. Rudolf Bultmann as quoted by David Van Biema, "The Gospel Truth?" *Time*, 8 April 1996, 54.

5. Robert W. Funk, Roy W. Hoover, and the Jesus Seminar, *The Five Gospels: What Did Jesus Really Say?* (New York: Scribner, 1993), 1.

6. Ibid.

7. James D. G. Dunn, *Jesus Remembered* (Grand Rapids: William. B. Eerdmans, 2003), 58.

8. N. T. Wright, "A Return to Christian Origins (Again)," *Bible Review*, December 1999, 10.

9. Funk, Hoover, and the Jesus Seminar, *The Five Gospels: What Did Jesus Really Say?*

10. Philip Jenkins, *Hidden Gospel: How the Search for Jesus Lost Its Way* (Oxford: Oxford University Press, USA, 2001), 5.

11. Harold Bloom, as quoted by Darrell Bock, interviewed by John Ankerberg on "Missing Gospels," program #1, *The John Ankerberg Show*.

12. Jenkins, *Hidden Gospel*, 13.

13. Bock, interview by Ankerberg, "Missing Gospels," program #6, *The John Ankerberg Show*.

14. Eckhard J. Schnabel, *Early Christian Mission—Jesus and the Twelve* (Downers Grove, IL: InterVarsity Press, 2004), 23.

15. John Piper, *God Is the Gospel* (Wheaton: Crossway, 2005), 54.

Lie #5: Jesus Has a Dark Secret

1. James D. Tabor, *The Jesus Dynasty* (New York: Simon and Schuster, 2006), 59.

2. Ibid., 234.

3. Ibid., 60.

4. Ibid.

5. Ibid., 61.

6. Ibid., 64.

7. Donald Carson interviewed by Martin Bashir, "Jesus Dynasty," *Nightline*, ABC News, 7 April 2006, copyright © ABC News Internet Ventures.

8. Ibid.

9. John Shelby Spong, *Born of a Woman: A Bishop Rethinks the Birth of Jesus* (San Francisco: HarperSanFrancisco, 1992).

10. Ibid., 18.

11. Ibid., 71.

12. John Shelby Spong, *Rescuing The Bible from Fundamentalism* (San Francisco: HarperSanFrancisco, 1991), 116–21.

13. Spong, *Born of a Woman,* 12.

14. N. T. Wright, *Who Was Jesus?* (Grand Rapids: William B. Eerdmans, 1992), 91.

15. Portions of this chapter were adapted from Erwin W. Lutzer, *Christ Among Other gods* (Chicago: Moody Press, 1994), chap. 4.

Lie #6: Jesus Is One Way among Many

1. Ann Oldenburg, "The divine Miss Winfrey?" *USA Today*, 11 May 2006, Life, sec. D.

2. Kathryn Lofton, professor at Reed College, quoted in "The divine Miss Winfrey?"

3. Cathleen Falsani, "There's no denying the power of 'the Oprah'," *Chicago Sun-Times*, 18 November 2005. Online version last accessed 5/4/07 at http://findarticles.com/ p/articles/mi_qn4155/is_20051118/ai_n15908544; also quoted in "The divine Miss Winfrey?"

4. Oldenburg, "The divine Miss Winfrey?"

5. Marcia Nelson, *The Gospel according to Oprah* (Louisville: Westminster John Knox Press, 2005), 57.

6. Patty Thomson, "Losing Teagan," *Bethel Focus* (Spring 2003), http://www.bethel.edu/ alumni/Focus/Spring/03/teagan.html last accessed 6/8/07.

7. LaTonya Taylor, "The Church of O," *Christianity Today*, 1 April 2002, 43.

8. Ibid., 39.

9. Roger Ebert, "Winfrey Confronts the Strength and the Spirits of 'Beloved'," *Chicago Sun-Times*, 11 October 1998. See http://rogerebert.suntimes.com/apps/pbc.dll/ article?AID=/19981011/PEOPLE/10010347/1023 last accessed 6/8/07.

10. Nelson, *The Gospel according to Oprah,* 83.

11. John Piper, *God Is the Gospel,* 13.

12. Al Mohler, "Now, Wait Just a Minute . . . When Is a Blurb Not a Blurb?" www.AlbertMohler.com (19 January 2006) http://www.albertmohler.com/blog_read. php?id=466, last accessed 4/18/2007.

13. "One way or many ways? The Gospel According to Oprah," Watchman Fellowship, transcribed from video clip. http://www.watchman.org/oprah.htm, last accessed 4/18/2007.

14. Cornelius Plantinga Jr., *Not the Way It's Supposed to Be: A Breviary of Sin* (Grand Rapids: William B. Eerdmans Pub. Co., 1995), xii.

15. Ibid., 100–101. Plantinga is quoting from Mary Midgley, *Can't We Make Moral Judgments?* (New York: St. Martin's Press, 1991), x.

16. Donald W. McCullough, *The Trivialization of God* (Colorado Springs: NavPress, 1995), 86.

17. Plantinga, *Not the Way It's Supposed to Be: A Breviary of Sin,* 8.

Finding a Jesus You Can Trust

1. Michael Baigent, *The Jesus Papers* (San Francisco: HarperCollins, 2006), 269–70.

2. For verification of these claims see Ron Rhodes, *Answering the Objections of Atheists, Agnostics, and Skeptics* (Eugene, OR: Harvest House, 2006), 123–53.

3. Paul W. Barnett, *Jesus and the Logic of History* (Downers Grove, IL: InterVarsity Press, 1997), 140.

4. Ibid., 138.

5. Stephen Neill, *Crises of Belief* (London: Hodder and Stoughton, 1984), 31.

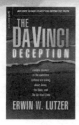